ANOTHER DAY,
ANOTHER DOLLAR

ANOTHER DAY,

By John T. Winterich

Philadelphia and New York

ANOTHER DOLLAR

Illustrated by Beatrice Tobias

J. B. LIPPINCOTT COMPANY

Acknowledgements

Of the material in this book, the following chapters originally appeared in *The New Yorker:* "Honesty, Etc.," "Eggs in One Basket," "All Things to All Men," "Save the Giblets," "The Incomplete Arsonist," "A Special Kind of Insult," and "Home-Town Stuff." "Clio and Aunt Bertha" was first published in *The Saturday Review of Literature.* I wish to express my gratitude to the staff of *The Providence Journal,* to the Providence Police Department, and to the office of Attorney General John H. Nolan of Rhode Island for invaluable help in the preparation of the account of the Bishop-Champlin murder case.

J. T. W.

Contents

Illustrations

How All This Started

O NE of the sillier things the Army asked me to do (or so it seemed at the time) was to GIVE A COMPLETE REC-ORD OF CIVILIAN EMPLOYMENT. START WITH YOUR LAST POSITION AND WORK BACK TO THE FIRST POSITION YOU HELD. DESCRIBE YOUR FIELD OF WORK AND POSITION AND STATE YOUR DUTIES AND RE-SPONSIBILITIES SO SPECIFICALLY AND IN SUCH DETAIL AS TO MAKE YOUR QUALIFICATIONS AS CLEAR AS POSSIBLE. "NAME OF EMPLOYER" SHOULD BE THE ORGANIZATION NAME, NOT THE OWNER'S OR SUPER-VISOR'S. "KIND OF BUSINESS OR ORGANIZATION" SHOULD BE SPECIFIED BY TYPE OF ESTABLISHMENT AND COMMODITY OR SERVICE (E.G., MANUFACTURER OF ELEVATORS, WHOLESALE FURNITURE). "NUMBER AND CLASS OF EMPLOYEES YOU SUPERVISED" SHOULD INDICATE WHETHER SUPERVISION WAS DIRECT OR INDIRECT. "EARNED INCOME" SHOULD NOT INCLUDE TRAVEL EXPENSE AND SIMILAR ITEMS. "EX-ACTLY WHAT YOU DID" SHOULD SHOW YOUR FUNCTION. IN ENGINEER-ING THIS WOULD BE CONSTRUCTION, DESIGN, OPERATION, ETC., IN INDUSTRY FUNCTION WOULD BE EXPRESSED AS SALES, PURCHASING, OVER-ALL MANAGEMENT, ACCOUNTING, ETC. IN OTHER OCCUPATIONS,

SIMILARLY, EXACT FUNCTIONS SHOULD BE STATED TO GIVE THE
CLEAREST POSSIBLE PICTURE OF YOUR EXPERIENCE.

This mandate, despite its seeming comprehensiveness, did not
touch my civilian career at a single point. I had never manu-
factured elevators, wholesaled furniture, or constructed, designed, or operated anything. I had never sold (except in bits
and pieces), never purchased beyond my own modest wants,
never over-all managed anybody or anything, never accounted
except to my conscience, and that not often enough.

I could understand why the Army might reasonably be interested in what I had been doing in 1940, but why should it be
concerned about what I had been doing in 1904? Yet WD AGO
Form 0857 demanded just that. It called for "a complete record
of civilian employment." I was required to "work back to the
first position" I had ever held.

Very well. If that was what WD AGO wanted, it should have
it. It is always best to take an Army order literally. Free-lance
interpretations of regulations are frowned upon. There are such
things as courts-martial. If the answers to Form 0857 appeared
flippant, the fault would not be mine. I recalled Tom Sawyer,
the cat Peter, and the Pain-Killer. "Now you've asked for it,"
says Tom, "and I'll give it to you, because there ain't anything
mean about me."

So I began setting down the data on a trial sheet, working in
chronological order—I could reverse the thing later. I had actually earned money at the age of eight or nine, but that was an
isolated job, not a "position." Then a while later a position was
more or less offered me when I should have become old enough
to accept it, but that was hardly a position attained, let alone
"held." "First position you held," as per WD AGO Form 0857,
came out like this:

PLACE (CITY) (STATE)	Providence, R.I.
FROM (MONTH AND YEAR) TO (MONTH AND YEAR)	? 1903–? 1904
NAME OF EMPLOYER	Benjamin F. Rich
ADDRESS	Broad and Calla Streets
KIND OF BUSINESS OR ORGAN- IZATION	Retail grocery
NUMBER AND CLASS OF EM- PLOYEES YOU SUPERVISED	None
MACHINES AND EQUIPMENT USED	Bicycle
EXACT TITLE OF POSITION	Delivery boy
EARNED INCOME (PER AN- NUM) FINAL	$52
EARNED INCOME (PER AN- NUM) STARTING	$52
EXACTLY WHAT DID YOU DO?	Delivered groceries

This looked as if it might be good fun. I fell to with a will. Eight or nine years sped by in such statistical detail as I could recall, and at last I was standing on the rear platform of a bouncing little eight-bench, open trolley car on the way to Hunt's Mills, a pleasant little dance and picnic resort a few miles east of Providence, slap up against the Massachusetts state line. Or, as I capsuled the matter for Form 0857:

PLACE (CITY) (STATE)	Providence, R.I., and vicinity
FROM (MONTH AND YEAR) TO (MONTH AND YEAR)	June 1912–September 1912
NAME OF EMPLOYER	Rhode Island Company
ADDRESS	Union Station
KIND OF BUSINESS OR ORGAN- IZATION	Street railway system

NUMBER AND CLASS OF EM-PLOYEES YOU SUPERVISED	One (motorman)
MACHINES AND EQUIPMENT USED	Trolley cars, fare-collector, transfer-punch, small change
EXACT TITLE OF POSITION	Trolley-car conductor
EARNED INCOME (PER AN-NUM) FINAL	$780
EARNED INCOME (PER AN-NUM) STARTING	$780
EXACTLY WHAT DID YOU DO?	Collected fares, punched and issued transfers, gave motorman starting and stopping signals, ejected drunks, reported accidents involving my car

I read over what I had set down and was fascinated by the result. Here was a complete record of my economic life from the age of twelve to the age of twenty-one. (I went on beyond that, of course, since the Army wanted the thing "complete," but my maturity is no concern of this book.) I could not see that my fiscal juvenilia would be of any use to the AGO at the moment, let alone to succeeding archivists, but the record held high significance for me, for

> . . . all experience is an arch wherethrough
> Gleams that untravell'd world whose margin fades
> For ever and for ever when I move.

And it occurred to me that anyone well along in adulthood must find a similar fascination in recollecting his own experiences as a youthful wage earner—or an earner, at least, of pocket money.

For nearly all of the take represented in the financial progression (with an occasional retrogression) chronicled in the pages that follow was mine to do with as I pleased. What it amounted to was that I earned my own allowance and, later on, my own clothes and my way through college. I could not have done this if my father and my stepmother had not boarded and lodged me free. I could not have afforded to go to college if I had had to go away from home, nor could my father have afforded to send me. Going to college in one's own town and living at home is the worst way in the world to go to college, but it is better than not going at all.

So I went from job to job as whim or opportunity suggested, having much more fun than if I had been doing nothing, and having plenty of time left for school, study, reading, play, plays, church, and modest but pleasant social activities. I would wish to avoid any nostalgia for "the good old days," though I certainly think that "free enterprise" was much freer and far more enterprising in my boyhood than it is today, when those who shout loudest about it will bear closest watching. My economic education was effected largely in an atmosphere of small business—in a little world of enterprising people who were out to do big things in a little way (and perhaps eventually in a big way), and of unenterprising people who were content merely to make both ends meet and to keep them met.

I do not feel called upon to vouch for the strict autobiographical authenticity of what follows. Memory is a kind of Milky Way, in which glowing patches of accuracy are bordered by black, bleak pits of utter forgetfulness or, worse, of defective or distorted recollection. In every instance I am reasonably certain that I have recalled correctly the amount of pay I got, which is as it should be in a personal economic history. If on occasion I have pointed up an incident, or guessed, or employed a spark of invention to bridge a dark gap, or become more interested in people encountered on the job than in the job itself, I trust that the reader will understand that my intentions have been of the best, and that the substratum of veracity remains unimpaired throughout, even where it is invisible.

II

Honesty, Etc.

IN the era just before the present century and myself had
reached our teens, the streets of Providence, Rhode Island,
like those of most of the rest of our cities, were illuminated
by two kinds of electric lights. What kind of light you got depended on what kind of street you lived on. Main thoroughfares
were served by arc lamps, which chewed at sticks of carbon with
a night-long sizzle and sputter. In the daytime a workman
climbed each arc-lamp pole, cranked the lamp back toward him
along the iron standard from which it hung until the big glass
globe was within his reach, pulled out the stub of carbon and
threw it to the street, inserted a fresh carbon stick, cranked the
lamp back to the end of the standard, and returned to earth. The
carbon stubs were legitimate jetsam for the youth of the vicinity,
who used them to draw portraits or to inscribe taunts on side-
walks. Occasionally the workman, who carried his fresh carbons
in a stout denim bag, would carelessly drop one, and apparently
it was against the code for him to pick it up. These unused sticks
were regarded by us children as trove of a superior order.

Less populous areas got their street illumination from incandescent bulbs at the ends of fixtures, modelled on the Ho-
garthian line of beauty, which curved gracefully out over the
street from green wooden poles. The tiny bulb at the end of the
fixture was something of an anticlimax. It gave just enough light
so that a footpad could pretty well determine the economic status
of a casual pedestrian as he was passing beneath it. Then, if he

looked worth picking, the footpad could loot him in security a hundred feet beyond. I do not know that this ever happened.

One of these exiguous lights glimmered nightly in front of the Vaughn house, on Babcock Street. Babcock Street started at Broad Street, almost opposite the Eighteens' firehouse, and petered out half a mile away, at the edge of Roger Williams Park. There were perhaps twenty houses along Babcock Street, most of them in the first three or four hundred feet. The Vaughns lived near the upper end of the more densely inhabited fraction of the street. They were father, mother, and four sons—Eugene, Ralph, Sidney, and Raymond—and they have no concern with this history beyond the accident of being friends of mine and living right behind an incandescent street light.

One afternoon, an hour or more after school was out, I stood in front of the Vaughn house waiting for Eugene or Ralph or Sidney, individually or in any combination, to come out and play. (Raymond was too young to count.) I do not know why I was not waiting in the house. Perhaps, like most persons of my age, I was something of a claustrophobe and, if I had any waiting to do, preferred the open sky.

I say "of my age," but I am uncertain just what my age was. I know that I was far enough along in arithmetic to encounter problems that did not come out even. Up to the end of the previous grade, if I were required to divide 186,063 by 327, I could take on the job in the assurance that the final dividend, however long delayed, would correspond exactly with the final divisor, and that if this consummation failed to come off, it was the fault not of the figures but of the figurer. Recently, however, I had been confronting problems that developed fuzzy and disagreeable fringes at the ends, if you could call them ends—dividing 327 not into 186,063 but into 186,603 or 186,306. Short of doing the business over again (or, of course, trusting to the teacher's verdict), there was no way of telling whether the result was ac-

The stone soared unaimed into the bulb and shattered it with a pop.

curate or not. Life, I had already decided, was a more lopsided and hit-or-miss business than I had been led to believe. I was due to get supporting data for this conviction within the next five minutes.

There was no curbstone in front of the Vaughn house; the ground simply slid into a shallow, gravelly gutter at the base of the light pole. I picked a handful of stones out of the gutter and began tossing them, one at a time, into a puddle a little way down the street. The target was so large and so near that the sport quickly palled, and by way of variety I raised my left leg and began flipping pebbles at nothing, under it. The torque imparted by the meeting of wrist and thigh, combined with the precarious balance of the thrower, lent to each missile a pleasantly erratic course. I could not tell what was going to happen. I could not tell, that is, until the last stone I have ever cast in this fashion soared unaimed into the incandescent bulb overhead and shattered it with a pop which, so far as I was concerned, proclaimed the end of the world.

I do not, I trust, have to explain that I was not trying to hit the bulb. I was not even trying to miss it. For the moment I had not even been conscious of the bulb's existence. If I had previously taken an oath not to stir from that spot until I had broken the bulb by this technique of subfemoral propulsion, I should probably be there to this day, well established as an eccentric of considerable repute, not unknown to Ripley, and afflicted with a permanent Charley horse in my left leg.

Babcock Street, as I have indicated, was not in a populous neighborhood and, since it went nowhere, was seldom used by anyone who was going anywhere. But within seconds after the disaster it was thronged. The throng consisted of two boys who came along the other side of the street. They were boys with whom I had only a nodding acquaintance, and any boy whom

one did not know well was, of course, thoroughly untrust-
worthy—certainly in a crisis of these dimensions.

"Nyah, nyah, *we* saw you!" screamed one of them.

"*You're* goin' to catch it!" cried the other.

"I didn't mean to," I explained. It was a useless and incredible
declaration, but I wanted to get it in the record. It seemed to
carry as little weight as I had expected.

"*You'll* catch it!" yelled the first boy.

"*We* saw you! *We* saw you!" said the other.

Therein lay the rub. Unquestionably they had seen me. Unquestionably, too, living in a neighborhood that depended for
its street illumination on this same type of light, they knew that
to every pole was affixed a printed notice which read,

$10 REWARD WILL BE PAID FOR INFORMATION LEADING TO
THE ARREST AND CONVICTION OF ANYONE BREAKING THIS LIGHT.
Narragansett Electric Lighting Company.

Or perhaps it was twenty dollars. Whichever it was, it was a
fabulous amount—a sum to gain which one would without
hesitation have turned in one's grandmother.

I sprinted for home. I assumed that in cases of this sort the
Narragansett Electric Lighting Company made the apprehension of the culprit the first order of business (which was not going to give them a great deal of trouble in the present instance);
that trial, conviction, and prison followed speedily; and that
the broken bulb was then replaced, with elaborate ceremony,
by way of warning.

There was one tiny ray of light in this terrible business, a light
no more powerful than that cast by the ineffectual incandescent
bulb itself when it had been in working order. The time was
nearly six o'clock. The lighting company's offices were closed
for the day, and the two witnesses could not pour their damning

intelligence into the proper ears before nine the following morning. If I could be there at the same time, or a little bit earlier, explain that the whole thing was an accident, and offer to make restitution, then all might conceivably yet be well. After all, the company would save ten dollars under such procedure, or twenty.

Luckily my father was home, and I told him the story and outlined my program. He listened gravely.

"We'll drive down there first thing in the morning," he said. "Don't worry about those two boys. Even if they hadn't seen you, if nobody in the world had seen you, if that light had been in the middle of the desert of Sahara, you would still have a moral obligation to pay the lighting people for the damage you did to their property. You see that, don't you?"

I nodded dutifully, and thought, but did not say, that it would be a threefold pleasure to write off a moral obligation, keep out of jail, and be in a position to thumb my nose at the two potential informants—all, as it were, with a single flip of the hand.

In the morning my father hitched up Selim and we drove downtown. The Narragansett Electric Lighting Company's offices were in Providence's only skyscraper, the twelve-story Union Trust Building. No sign of the two gleeful witnesses in the entrance hallway, no sign of them in the elevator. Best of all, no sign of them in the lighting company's offices when my father opened the door and I followed him fearfully in. My terror subsided considerably, but not altogether; the witnesses might even now be closeted with the president.

"This young man broke one of your incandescent street lights by accident," my father explained to a pompadoured young lady who beamed at me across the counter as if light breakers were her private failing. "He wants to pay for it."

"Just a moment," she said. "I'll call the manager."

The manager looked to be of sterner stuff than the pompadoured lady. No beams out of him. But the close attention he gave to my father's narrative, which pictured me as the most contrite resident of Providence at that precise moment (and made no mention of any witnesses to my deed), indicated pretty clearly that the incident had not yet been brought to his notice. At the end of my father's recital, the manager turned his gaze on me. He rubbed his chin with his right hand, and I could just hear the little hiss as his fingers passed across a few bristles that had escaped his razor.

"Hmmm," he said very slowly and judicially. "I see. I see." Then, having made up his mind, he went on briskly, "Customarily, in a situation of this kind, there would be a charge of seventy-five cents for the light and an additional charge of seventy-five cents for the labor of installing it. But you have been so straight and honest in coming here right away and telling us about what happened that it's not going to cost you anything. And when you're a few years older and start looking for a job, you come down here and this company will give you one."

The Narragansett Electric Lighting Company dropped the "Lighting" out of its name some twenty-five years later, in consideration of the vacuum cleaners and washing machines and hair curlers and juice extractors that were undreamed of in an earlier and innocent day. I never accepted the manager's offer. I just happened to take up something else. But I think it only fair (and perfectly safe) to lay the facts before the present president of the company and to tell him I am sure he is doing as well with Narragansett Electric as I would have done.

Eggs in One Basket

THE first salaried job I ever had—the salary was one dollar a week—was as boy of all work for Benjamin Franklin Rich, who operated an infinitesimal grocery at the southwest corner of Broad and Calla Streets in Providence. My duties in no wise interfered with my education, for I started work at seven in the morning and was always through in plenty of time to be at my desk in Broad Street Grammar School, a couple of hundred yards from the grocery, before class convened.

Benjamin Franklin Rich was a Cape Codder. I have no idea why he abandoned the Cape for Providence. He was a huge, stolid, silent, slow-moving creature, with shaggy eyebrows and a full beard. He looked like a bust of Homer on whose head some prankster had set a hat. I cannot recall ever seeing him with his hat off except in church. Like me, Mr. Rich was a faithful attendant at Washington Park Methodist.

He had almost no voice. He spoke in a low, throaty rumble that seemed to tangle in his beard. The words came out barely audible and, unless one was used to the rumble, scarcely intelligible. I worked for him, I think, the better part of a year—I constituted his entire staff, as a matter of fact—but I cannot recall a single scrap of any of the conversations that must have taken place between us every day.

I have no memory even of the circumstances under which I was engaged, though certainly that process must have involved some conversation. I see myself only *in medias res,* pedalling a five-dollar secondhand bicycle from the store down into Washington Park in the mornings to find out what the Methodist minister and one or two other special customers wanted to order.

Methodist ministers were moved around like checkers in that day, and during the period I was working for Mr. Rich a new one was assigned to our church. I was instructed to inform him of the excellence of Mr. Rich's wares and of the regularity and punctuality of his delivery system. I landed him. This remains my supreme achievement in the field of salesmanship.

The ways of Providence—I mean the Providence for whom Providence, Rhode Island, was named—pass understanding, but there are occasions, I am sure, when it operates with calculated irony. For it was in this milieu of evangelistic piety and rugged fundamentalism that I was given my first glimpse into the awful depths of human depravity.

Our customers, for the most part, lived in unbeautiful houses, usually two or three families to a house; they dressed tastelessly, and they ate plain food. One of them, a Mrs. D——, was among the more rhapsodic communicants at the Methodist church. She was at the forefront in any religious activity that called for emotion and noise. The new minister, an English-born mill hand who had seen a great light, was strong on salvation, conversion, testimony, revivals, and related manifestations. This sort of business was right up Mrs. D——'s street. She not only put on a good show in prayer meeting, she talked church at every opportunity. Mr. Rich offered a splendid opportunity. He did not go in for ecclesiastical fireworks, but he was a devout worshipper and a worthy fellow-laborer in the vineyard, and he listened better than he talked.

One cold winter morning, after I had completed my rounds, I was hanging around the tiny store getting warmed up before I set out for school. On the counter was a shallow wicker basket containing perhaps three dozen eggs. My eye caught a pencil

mark on one of them. I picked the egg up and saw that someone
had started to sketch a face on the shell. It was a rather good
face, or was on the way to being one, but the portraitist had
evidently decided that there was something he was better at or
that there were better things than eggs to draw on. I put the egg
down.

The door opened and Mrs. D—— came in. "Brrr!" she said.
"Snappy."

Mr. Rich, who was reading the morning paper, rumbled a
presumable affirmation.

"All I want now is a pound of lard," said Mrs. D——. "I'll be
back by-and-by for some other things."

Mr. Rich lumbered toward the icebox, and Mrs. D——, who
was standing at the counter beside the basket of eggs, asked him
if he didn't think the services last Sunday evening had been
lovely and if he didn't think the services next Sunday evening
would be lovely. From the depths of the icebox, Mr. Rich agreed
with her. I turned and rubbed a hole in the frost on the window
to see what was going on outside.

Mrs. D—— prattled on and Mr. Rich answered unintelligibly
as he scraped the lard off the long wooden spatula he was using
into a container made of thin wood. As I turned back from the
window he was finishing this operation. He wrapped the package and tied it undeftly. Mrs. D—— paid for the lard. As she
started out, I opened the door for her and she said, "Thank you,
my dear."

There was still a little time to kill before I needed to start for
school, and I got to thinking about the egg. It seemed to me the
drawing was better than I could have done. I wondered again
why the unknown artist hadn't finished the job—hair, collar,
necktie, even spectacles and a beard. A competent hand could
readily transform it into a likeness of Mr. Rich. I went over the
whole basket, scanning every egg all the way around and segre-

She asked Mr. Rich if he didn't think the services last Sunday
had been lovely.

gating the examined eggs from the rest. The marked egg was not there.

I never told Mr. Rich. I don't know why I didn't. A misapplied sense of chivalry, perhaps, or a timid adherence to the principle of you-better-keep-out-of-this. But I wish I had counted the eggs—though of course there was no reason to—when I noticed the sketch. I have often wondered whether any of the unmarked ones were also missing.

IV

Door to Door

ALETTER CARRIER named Reuben Weeks used to
live near our house. He was tall, spare, redheaded,
soft of speech, and gentle of soul. When he finished
delivering mail he used to change his clothes and go to another part of town and sell water filters from house to house,
either for the extra money there was in it or in order to complete more quickly that trip to the moon which every letter
carrier, even today, can make if he will only put his mind and
feet to it.

The water filters Mr. Weeks sold were no more complicated
than a five-and-ten-cent-store squirt gun and operated on much
the same principle, as Mr. Weeks demonstrated to me one evening. They came in two types, one threaded, for threaded
faucets, and one plain, with a rubber neckpiece, for plain faucets.
Each filter contained two discs of screen wire of fairly fine mesh,
and this was all there was to the filtering business. As a prophy-
lactic device the filter was probably about as effective as a stove
grate, but it did channel the flow of water into a smooth, silent
stream, which was a matter of some importance in a day when,
for whatever reason, the ordinary kitchen tap discharged its contents like the Bridal Veil Falls.

"Women don't like to get splashed," Mr. Weeks explained.

The filters sold for ten cents each, and Mr. Weeks was allowed
to keep half of that as his commission.

"Why don't you try your luck?" Mr. Weeks asked me one day.

"Providence is a pretty big place. Room enough for everybody."

I thought it was a great idea. At Mr. Weeks's suggestion I filled my right jacket pocket with threaded filters and the left with plain ones. This gave me a rather bunchy appearance, but it left my hands empty, which was a great advantage to a door-to-door salesman, Mr. Weeks said, because housewives reasoned that a stranger who wasn't carrying anything couldn't be selling anything, and doors that would otherwise have remained closed were readily opened.

I selected an area in South Providence which no one had yet taken over, where most of the dwellings were two- and three-family affairs. The technique of filter selling, as Mr. Weeks expounded it, was simple. When the lady of the house came to the door the demonstrator showed her a threaded filter and asked her if she would let him attach it to the kitchen faucet and leave it overnight without any obligation on her part. The threaded filter was shown first because every house or tenement had a cold-water tap, naturally. If the tenants were well-to-do two-tap people, the demonstrator would bring out a plain-faucet filter, once he was in the place, and affix that too. If the lady of the house liked the filter, or filters, then on the following day she would pay the demonstrator. Otherwise he took the filters back and no hard feelings.

I should estimate that about half the people who opened their doors to me let me leave filters, and that, of these, at least half paid out their dimes the next day. Thus one sale to every four visits was a virtual certainty—you could look down a street, count the houses, and compute what you were going to get almost to the exact cent. I am not an expert in these matters, but experienced canvassers have since told me that this one-in-four ratio is exceedingly high, and that if the filters had sold for ten dollars each I should have quickly become wealthy, and in the zeal for even greater wealth I should probably have had

On perhaps his thirtieth try Charlie got his feet into the air and
held them there.

a nervous and physical breakdown, and died much younger than I shall.

As it was, by working an hour or so every day after school and three or four hours on Saturday I was soon making a dollar and a half or sometimes two dollars a week, and this in a day when from two to three dollars was the standard wage for most beginning jobs for youngsters working full time.

I recall no adventures, or even misadventures, in my few weeks as a filter salesman—no doors slammed in my face, no attempts to gyp me out of my dime by brazenly denying I had left a filter, or even by just not being home. That, I should say, was another advantage of a ten-cent filter over a ten-dollar filter. I ran into people who spoke little English, but they didn't have to speak English to appreciate a nice, clean, splashless kitchen sink, and they understood ten cents.

Sometimes the threaded filter wouldn't fit tightly enough and two or three little geysers would bubble out over the edges, threatening a no-sale. The technique in this situation was for the demonstrator to cluck his tongue over the deplorable state of the faucet threads, take a length of ordinary twine from his pocket, wrap it around the faucet threads, screw the filter on again, and hope that the flow of water would now keep within channels. Usually it did. It was generally safe during this procedure to keep up the patter about the condition of the faucet, because these were mainly rented tenements, and a landlord was always fair game. Instead of doing harm, therefore, the disparagement actually built up a sympathetic understanding between seller and buyer, and almost always a sale followed.

It was fun to be getting rich the way I was, but I was beginning to suffer, along with all this cash in pocket, the ineluctable penalty of riches—loneliness. It occurred to me that it would be fun to have a companion, he to take one side of a street and I the other. We could call out our failures and successes to each other, and anything else that came to our minds, as things were bound to. Providence, as Mr. Weeks had remarked, was a pretty big place.

I approached as a desirable collaborator a crony named Charlie who could do simple card tricks, yodel, and stand on his hands for a second or two once in a dozen tries. While no one of these specialties earmarked Charlie as bound to succeed in the filter business, I felt that such versatility was certainly not a factor to ignore. This turned out to be a shrewd bit of character analysis on my part, or something like that.

Charlie was enthusiastic over my suggestion. So at half-past nine the following Saturday morning we started down a brand-new street, he on the south side and I on the north. By noon I had left twenty-one filters and Charlie seventeen—we were really about even, because he had two or three more vacant lots on his side than I had on mine. I suggested we knock off then, because housewives do not like to be disturbed when they are preparing a meal or eating it, and Saturday afternoon was bad because so many people went down street to the stores.

Monday afternoon after school we went back to collect dimes or filters. Thirteen of my twenty-one customers and ten of Charlie's seventeen paid their dimes and kept the filters. Next afternoon we were about even on the number of filters left, and on Wednesday our collections were approximately the same. On Thursday we distributed again and on Friday we collected.

At this point the collection curve on Charlie's sales chart, if he had been keeping one, would have recorded a big spurt upward. I have forgotten how many filters he had planted on Thursday, but on Friday he collected for all but one of these.

On Saturday morning we got going soon after eight o'clock and put in an intensive four hours of distribution. I left thirty-three filters and Charlie thirty-four—a record for each of us.

On Monday I collected on nineteen of these and Charlie on thirty-two.

We reported to Mr. Weeks one or two evenings a week, turned in our money, obtained fresh supplies, and swapped experiences. At our next meeting Charlie, who was usually pretty much of a chatterbox, had nothing to contribute in the way of experiences, although both Mr. Weeks and I hinted rather broadly that we could do with an explanation of the sudden rise in Charlie's sales ratio. Charlie affected to believe that his showing was in no way remarkable, but we knew he knew better, and he knew we knew he knew better.

During the next couple of weeks Charlie's sales curve remained at a consistently high level—it was, in fact, a curve no longer but a lofty plateau. While I was putting forth exactly the same effort that Charlie was, I was earning only about half as much. It was pretty discouraging. Moreover the circle of our activities was spreading farther afield; it was more of a chore to get to the scene of action, and very much more of a chore to get home again. The easy money was turning tough. I decided it was high time to take a rest, or to look around for something else.

My depression hit bottom at the close of business one collecting afternoon when Charlie had me licked exactly three to one —twenty-seven sales to my nine. Charlie, of course, was jubilant. He attempted to stand on his hands every few feet. And then, as we passed the greensward of Roger Williams Park where it touches Broad Street, a miracle befell. On perhaps his thirtieth try at handstanding Charlie got his feet into the air and held them there. I cheered—the acrobat, not the salesman. For what seemed minutes Charlie remained almost as rigid as a statue— a statue upside down. Then something moved—something that was not Charlie. A small flat tin can which had probably once held snuff or shoe polish fell out of his pants' pocket. It bounced off the ground and the cover came off, disclosing a quantity of tiny, curly green worms that wriggled in an ecstasy of bewilderment at their sudden and unlooked-for liberation.

Charlie's feet came down with a bump. Sheepishly he began picking up worms and putting them back in the tin. But something besides the worms was out. It was the secret of Charlie's success as a filter salesman. What housewife could resist investing ten cents in a device that would keep those awful little green things from getting into the teakettle?

Would I have employed this ruse if it had occurred to me? I don't know. It didn't occur to me, it occurred to Charlie. Reflecting on the episode occasionally in the years that have intervened, I have reached the conclusion that morality frequently may be just another name for lack of imagination.

V

All Things to All Men

MY brief affiliation with Benjamin Green's haberdashery was effected by answering a want ad in the
Providence Journal. Some twenty other youngsters
had the same idea, which was to work for Mr. Green every
Saturday from eight in the morning until ten at night for one
dollar. I got the job—because personality and charm stuck out
all over me, I like to think, but probably because my face was
clean and I wore a clean shirt and, perhaps most important of
all, a necktie.

"All right, now, the rest of you," Mr. Green said, clapping
his hands at my late competitors as if he were shooing chickens.
"Just clear out, now. No blocking up the aisles there, if you
please." There was only one aisle, but he said "aisles."

The platoon of the unemployed squeezed through the doorway, tossing back an assortment of scowls which were im-
partially apportioned between Mr. Green and myself. Not altogether by accident, a husky straggler upset a pile of dollar shirts,
size 16½. I began my duties by picking them off the floor.
Mr. Green helped. When we stood up, he said, "Your name
is—" as if he knew it but it had slipped his mind.

I told him.

"Now, that's rather a difficult name," he said. "In this business—in almost any business, but especially in this business—
people want names that are easy to say and remember. You
don't think for a minute my name is really Green, do you?"

For some two hours—ever since I had bought that morning's paper and read his appeal—I most certainly had thought his name was Green. His question seemed to demand a ringing negative in response, but there might be a catch to that, so I merely looked noncommittal and confused, which was easy.

"You're absolutely right," said Mr. Green, just as though I *had* given him a ringing negative. "Green is an easy name to say and Green is an easy name to remember. If a person buys a necktie from us and a friend admires it and asks him where did he get it, it's easy for him to remember and say Green's. Same thing if the person wants another necktie for himself—he remembers he bought the first one at Green's. Here at Green's you will be Mr. Williams."

I blinked at the sound of this, my first and, to the date of this writing, only alias, and Mr. Green must have noticed my dismay.

"Oh, it's a good name, an honored name," he said, and added, "especially here in Rhode Island. Now," he went on after a pause during which he appeared to be reviewing the whole pageant of Colonial history, "I want you to come out to the stock room with me and unpack shirts."

I expected him to add, "Mr. Williams," but he didn't. During the dozen or so Saturdays I worked for Mr. Green, he never once addressed me directly as Mr. Williams. It took me some time to discover that while Mr. Williams and I were occasionally one and the same, at other times Mr. Williams was merely a creature of Mr. Green's luxuriant imagination. Mr. Williams, it became clear as Saturday succeeded Saturday, was sales manager, buyer, director of personnel, adjuster of grievances, bouncer, confidential messenger, janitor, chairman of the board, chief clerk, accountant, rectifier (and occasional perpetrator) of errors, whipping boy, scapegoat, tackling dummy, general factotum, or tutelary deity, as the situation demanded.

We went out to the stock room and Mr. Green showed me several boxes of shirts. I carried a batch of them out front and stacked them on the display counter. While I was carrying out a second batch, a woman wearing a fox neckpiece and a tall hat with crimson feathers came into the shop.

"Meet Mrs. Green," said Mr. Green, who had followed me out from the stock room with more shirts. "Mrs. Green, this is our new Saturday special."

Mrs. Green shook hands and smiled a gold-and-ivory smile. She asked me for my out-of-store name and said she would call me Jackie. She was tall, broad, and blonde, and tended to creak when she walked, which was seldom, for as soon as she had taken off the fox and the hat, she climbed onto a high stool in front of the cash register and was set for the day. She was not bad-looking; indeed, to my untutored eye she was ravishingly beautiful, but in this I may have been influenced by the fact that she was one of the kindest persons I have ever met.

"Don't rush so," she told me that first Saturday as I passed the cash register, and "Take it easy," and "Slow up, Jackie, there ain't any fire. Not here, anyways." Once, on a subsequent Saturday, when the too speedy consumption of a pound of cream peppermints had given me a slight queasiness, she made me lie down on a couch behind a rack of raincoats. When Mr. Green looked for me to run an errand, she told him she had sent me on one of her own.

The cash register over which Mrs. Green presided was at the end of a tiny counter which jutted out at right angles to the only less tiny main counter. Mrs. Green's flaxen locks rose up out of the cotton goods stacked round about her like a lighthouse at the tip of a sandspit. Beyond the jut of counter and the cash register was the stock room, a dark and cavernous area to which a modicum of light was admitted when the side door was opened. Outside the door was a dingy alleyway which bore the unlikely

I thought we must have taken on another employee.

designation of Empire Street. Since the store was on a corner, it could have had a side window, but a side window facing Empire Street would not have added to the reputation of the establishment. So it had only a front window.

There was only one employee besides myself—a slim-waisted youth named Eric who was the soul of courtliness to all female customers, without discrimination as to age, looks, color, or economic status. Eric was a full-time employee—a career man. He was twenty-two or twenty-three, I suppose—that is, at the peak of maturity.

That first Saturday morning wore on placidly. My job did not call for any great physical exertion, and it was clean work, involving in the main the unpacking, sorting, and arranging of quantities of shirts, socks, underwear, handkerchiefs, neckties, collars—especially collars, for in those days a man who wore a collar-attached shirt was assumed to be either a water-colorist or an adherent of Eugene V. Debs, or perhaps both.

The assistance of Mr. Williams was not required until a minute or two before eleven o'clock, when five customers, all apparently bent on catching an eleven-thirty-five train, stampeded into the store.

"Mr. Williams!" Mr. Green shouted gaily. "Oh, Mr. Williams!"

I was directly behind Mr. Green scooping up some empty collar boxes. I was about to go around in front of him to find out what he wanted when Mrs. Green called from her stool, "I sent Mr. Williams to the bank for some singles and silver. He'll be right back."

Mrs. Green, then, was privy to the Williams conspiracy, and could play up to it in such an emergency as this.

Mr. Green fumed about the matter to the two customers he was looking after; Eric was dealing with the others. Seven twenty-dollar bills already that morning, he complained. Seemed like a put-up job. Twenty-dollar bills looked mighty nice in the till, but they certainly ate up the small stuff.

The two customers paid for their purchases with the exact change and departed. Mr. Green took over one of Eric's three customers, and the crisis had been met.

Not until midafternoon did it become necessary to call on Mr. Williams to grapple with a second emergency. A big, red-faced man with a series of chins found to his delight that Mr. Green had a dozen balbriggan union suits of his calibre, and bought the lot.

"Have those sent over to the Crown Hotel, will you?" he said.

"We certainly will, sir," Mr. Green replied. "Mr. Williams will take them over immediately he returns from a rather late lunch. Thank *you,* sir." This time, of course, I became Mr. Williams and delivered a mountain of union suits to the Crown Hotel, where a bellhop took charge of them with alacrity and a dirty look.

Before closing time that evening, Mr. Williams had on several occasions justified his right to a name. At seven-thirty, when the store was more heavily populated than at any previous time during the day, Mr. Williams turned out to be dawdling over his dinner, and Mr. Green hinted that drastic action would be taken on his return. This tended to make disgruntled customers feel responsible for any misfortune that might overtake Mr. Williams, and they waited their turns patiently.

An hour later, Mr. Williams, this time in the flesh, was sent to another hotel with a load of shirts. Taking a leaf from the book of his opposite number, he dawdled over a five-cent ice-cream soda on the way back.

Just before closing time, a large, unkempt, coaly creature exuding whiskey and belligerence stumbled into the premises and began examining the texture of some dollar shirts with a rasping thumb and forefinger.

"I'm afraid we haven't anything in your line, my friend," Mr. Green said blandly.

"Oh, you ain't?"

"You're not going to use language like that in here!" Mr. Green cried, running to the side door. "Oh, Officer Williams! Will you just step in here a moment, please? A situation has arisen—" He turned back into the store. The ape man had gone.

I went home that first Saturday night certain that I was going to like the gents' furnishings business. As Saturday followed Saturday, this conviction was strengthened. Mr. Green was no more demanding than he had been on the first day, Mrs. Green no less kindly and affable. Eric asked me about school and was impressed, not altogether favorably, by my announcement that I was well into the first book of Caesar's *Gallic Wars*. "I only went through decimals and then I quit," he told me. "You got decimals and you got all you need in this business."

Mr. Williams, who was seemingly anything from a gentleman of vast intellectual resources and superlative administrative ability down to a gibbering Mongoloid, continued to play his part in the functioning of the establishment. Mr. Green was a devout believer in what a subsequent generation was to call the buildup. Mr. Williams was by no means all of the buildup. The shop, tiny as it was, was none the less divided into departments, though it would have been readily possible for a man of average height to have fallen from the neckware department clear across the hosiery department into the pajama department. Any package, incoming or outgoing, regardless of size, was a shipment. Mr. Green never said "most customers"; it was always "a vast majority of our clientele," rhyming it with "heel." Whenever Eric climbed into the modest window to rearrange the display, Mr. Green, in talking to any of our clientele who happened to be present, would invariably work in an allusion to "our window dresser." He never said, "I don't have that"; it was always "We don't have that"—and what we did have was always "better." It was never "the shop" or "store" but always "the house."

I, too, was caught in the thralldom of the buildup. Gradually I came to identify myself with Mr. Williams, always in his beneficent and constructive aspects. I selected a redoubtable Victorian mansion on Elmwood Avenue and peopled it with a complete Williams household—wife, son, daughter, parlormaid, cook, coachman. Mr. Williams himself was a gentleman of thirty-five, tall, distinguished alike in appearance and in deportment. He wore a frock coat and a dark blue necktie pierced with a lustrous pearl stickpin. His hair was black and abundant. So was his mustache. He spoke with the tongue of an angel and rarely used a word of fewer than three syllables. I thought he had an excellent chance of becoming President of the United States.

It was Mr. Green's very infatuation with buildup which produced the crisis that terminated my connection with the house, although Mr. Green himself never knew there had been a crisis. One Saturday evening, a man of perhaps forty, far more gaudily dressed than most of our patrons, entered the store, followed by a youngster who was obviously his son and who carried his nose as if he were pushing unpleasant smells aside with it.

The youth's eye, it appeared, had been taken by a necktie in the window. Mr. Green smiled and shook his head in admiration, as who would say, "I knew some individual of flawless taste would speedily discover *that* masterpiece." He climbed into the window to get it and stayed there several minutes. This was a maneuver to give the boy time to get interested in something more and also to give the father an opportunity to look around. But the boy quickly dismissed Mrs. Green and Eric from his attention and centered his inspection on me. I was standing near the cash register. He didn't like me and I didn't like him, and he flung down the gauntlet by sticking out his tongue at me.

Mr. Green emerged from the window, carrying the tie as if it were a priceless tapestry. The father gave him a ten-dollar bill. Normally, Mr. Green would have walked over to the cash register with this himself—it was about twenty feet away—but not when he had a chance like this. "Boy!" he called. "Cash boy!"

For a few brief seconds I thought we must have taken on another employee without my having been told about it. Then the incredible truth hit me. My *amour-propre* was being sacrificed to the Green delusion of grandeur. It became apparent, in one vivid, all-clarifying flash, that self-respect, except perhaps his own, meant nothing at all to Mr. Green. For the cash boy was the untouchable of retail merchandising. Only the big shops—department stores and such—employed cash boys. There, during busy periods, they could be seen hurrying around at the importunate beck of salesfolk. To switch from cash boy to anything else was a promotion.

"Cash boy!" Mr. Green called again, a little louder.

As I walked toward him, the obnoxious youngster hustled to get behind his father. He had nothing to fear from me, however; my archfoe, my only foe, was Mr. Green. I took the ten-dollar bill and walked slowly back to the cash register. Mr. Green didn't mind the slow pace—in fact, it fitted right in with the project.

"You feelin' all right, Jackie?" Mrs. Green asked.

I nodded. No need to drag a noble woman like that into the mess. I could have kicked Mr. Green in the shins and run, but, whatever his shortcomings, he was Mrs. Green's husband. Besides, in half an hour he would be owing me a dollar.

I got the change from Mrs. Green and took it back to Mr. Green, who was growing ecstatic over the sock display. The father put his money in his pocket, and he and the boy left the store.

At ten o'clock I collected my dollar from Mrs. Green and bade her and Eric an elaborate good night. I was resolved never to enter the place again, and I never did. An uneasy conscience, however, plus my liking for Mrs. Green, an innocent and ill-matched wife, impelled me to write Mr. Green a note a few days later saying I would be unable to work for him any more. I posted the letter so that he would get it the first thing Saturday morning.

VI

Everything for the Kitchen

THE Manufacturers' Outlet Company was (and still is) a large department store lining most of one side of Weybosset Street. In my early teens I had no trouble getting a Saturday job there, and a rather easy and pleasant job it was. The one drawback was that it paid only seventy-five cents.

I was assigned to Department AA—kitchen goods. My duties comprised principally the unpacking of pots and pans which I arranged on shelves and counters. There were half a dozen or so of us in AA—salesmen and saleswomen and the head of the department, Henry Healey, a short, plump, bald, perpetually good-natured man, brisk of movement, quick of speech, with an air of unassumed dignity about him. I never knew him to find fault with anyone in AA. He did not have to work at being a boss.

Everyone in the department seemed to be competent and efficient and to enjoy working with Mr. Healey. When I say competent and efficient I include, of course, myself. I had official if informal confirmation of this. Department AA was tucked into a corner of the Outlet basement, and this gave us a relative and appreciated privacy. One Saturday morning I was stacking a shipment of saucepans when a floorwalker (no carnation) strolled in and began passing the time of day with Hr. Healey. Being a floorwalker, he automatically let his eye rove over the department as he talked. It came to rest on me.

"Well, Henry, this stock boy of yours seems to keep sawing wood without making much noise about it," he said.

46

"John's a good boy—good worker," confirmed Mr. Healey.

I was, of course, immensely flattered. To be praised for industriousness was pleasant, but to be credited with the golden virtue of silence was positively dazzling. It had never happened to me before, it has never happened since, and I am afraid it will never happen again.

At the same time, the dual indorsement rankled a little. If I was that good I was worth more than seventy-five cents. I had previously held two jobs in mercantile establishments that paid me a dollar a week—the one at Benjamin Green's haberdashery had occupied the identical hours and, substituting shirts for kitchenware, had embraced identical duties. My acceptance of the seventy-five-cent job involved a loss of prestige. It also involved a loss of twenty-five cents a week.

I proposed to do something about it. Mr. Healey, I knew, had nothing to do with the amount of pay I was getting. Neither did the floorwalker. The figure was set by the superintendent of the store, whom I had never seen and whose name escapes me. He never came to Department AA while I was there. In fact, I do not remember ever seeing him on the floor at all.

This august being occupied an office halfway up the broad stairway at the rear of the main floor. Here he could look out over the bustle below like Napoleon at Ratisbon. It seemed to me, indeed, that he and Napoleon had quite a lot in common, though from the little I had read about him Napoleon seemed to me to have been somewhat more approachable.

Everything was running smoothly in Department AA, and that was just the trouble. I knew that there was no chance of advancement in Mr. Healey's little cosmos, and I was sure that, if there had been, Mr. Healey would have done something about it. There was nothing for it but to go direct to the superintendent.

I decided that early in the week (say Tuesday after school)

would be the best time to do this. In this way I could approach the superintendent with a certain detachment—as a more or less free agent who was separated from the superintendent's immediate dominion by a round half a week in each direction.

I walked up the stairs quietly and in good order. The door of the superintendent's office was open. He was busy with some papers—the payroll, perhaps. He heard me and looked up.

"Yes?"

"I work Saturdays in Department AA," I explained, and gave him my name. "I'm getting seventy-five cents, and I think I'm worth a dollar."

"I'll look into it," he said, and returned to his papers.

The interview had been brief enough, in all conscience, but I could not see that it had gone otherwise than satisfactorily—as satisfactorily as possible, short of having a raise promised me on the spot. He had not said no, or "If you don't think seventy-five cents is enough, go somewhere else." He would "look into it," and any just man, by looking into it, would quickly see that I was a bargain at a dollar.

We got our pay late Saturday evenings, just before closing time, by going over to a cashier's window on our floor. The following Saturday the cashier handed me an envelope which gave out no clink as she pushed it across her little counter. (A half dollar and a quarter in the same envelope will invariably clink when the envelope is jiggled.) I picked up the envelope and shook it. It was delightfully light and there was no clink. The phrase "folding money" had no currency at the time, at least in New England, but I never hear it today without a flashback of recollection to that Outlet dollar. (It was a dollar, all right.) It represented a three-way victory—a triumph of salesmanship, an appreciation of true worth, and twenty-five cents more a week.

On the next Saturday I performed prodigies for Mr. Healey. Around a quarter to ten that evening I walked confidently to

I was assigned to Department AA—kitchen goods.

the cashier's window. She pushed out an envelope. It clinked. Two half-dollars, doubtless. Nevertheless I ripped the envelope open with forebodings of disaster. These were immediately confirmed. One half-dollar and one quarter.

"Are you sure this is correct?" I asked the cashier, extending the two miserable coins for her examination.

She looked at her records.

"That's correct."

"Last week I got a dollar."

"I don't have last week's payroll here. You better see the superintendent."

I shot up the staircase to the main floor and then on up to the superintendent's watchtower of an office. I was in no mood to be trifled with—at that instant I should have been happy to take on both the superintendent *and* Napoleon. This spirit of no-compromise-with-injustice lasted precisely up to the moment I walked into his office. He was looking out over the main floor and his back was toward me. When he heard me he turned and faced me, with his eyebrows raised slightly in inquiry. Otherwise he was strictly dead-pan.

"I've been getting seventy-five cents a Saturday," I said. "About ten days ago I came to see you and said I thought I was worth a dollar. You told me you would look into it. The next Saturday—a week ago today—I got a dollar. Tonight I got seventy-five cents again."

"Must have been a mistake," he said, turning his back to look out over the store.

Then and there I missed my grand opportunity. I should have taken a quarter out of my pocket, banged it down on the desk, and told him what he could do with it. Well, not that exactly. A little irony would have been far more effective. "Oh, I beg your pardon, sir. In that case allow me to refund you the excess twenty-five cents. I trust this mistake" (strong accent on "mistake," which would have been uttered *larghetto*) "has not caused you or the company any inconvenience." Of course I would have been fired on the spot, but what a glorious dividend of satisfaction I should have had by way of compensation! Then, again, perhaps the superintendent would have seen that he had a man of mettle here. "Now wait a minute—wait a minute. Let's not be hasty about this. Feel you're equal to something better than stock boy in AA? Look in during the week and we'll talk things over. Always room at the Outlet for a person of initiative and spirit."

I did neither of these things. Without a word I went out, got my hat, and bade Mr. Healey and my fellow-toilers in AA good night. On the way home I seethed with a resolve to go to the store Monday. Or Tuesday. Or Wednesday. I would work up a good act—something with enough variant readings to block every argumentative hole into which the rat might try to scuttle. But by the time I reached home I knew that this would never be. I had let the climactic moment slip past me, and it would not come my way again. Out of this experience I coined a maxim, "Strike while the iron is hot," which has since attained considerable popularity.

VII

Save the Giblets

THE first time clock I ever punched was in the Providence Public Market. My number was 283. I worked in the market on Fridays after school and on Saturdays from seven in the morning until eleven at night. I got a dollar and sixty-five cents each week.

Mr. Swanson was president of the company. Mr. Senior was superintendent, and his assistant was Mr. Sutherland. (There may have been some ritualistic implication in all that *S* business in the higher administrative strata.) Either Mr. Senior or Mr. Sutherland was always on the floor, clad in a long white coat. Mr. Sutherland was tall and large framed, and his white coat tended to give him the aspect of a friar caught in a blizzard. We all wore white coats, for that matter, and the shoes we cared least about.

The Friday-Saturday help were assigned whatever jobs were augmented by the week-end rush. On Friday afternoons many of us were sent to the shipping room. A customer who wanted his order delivered would secure a long yellow blank form called a "traveler," and carry it from counter to counter as he made his purchases. Every traveler bore a separate number, and each clerk who made a traveler sale would write the number on the purchase and then toss the package onto one of a series of overhead belts which fed into a huge master belt that carried the goods upstairs to the shipping room. At the head of this con-

veyor a boy was stationed. It was his job to separate the numbered packages into odd and even, putting the odd (as I remember) on an auxiliary belt at his right and the even on a belt at his
left. Other boys stationed along these two lines removed the
parcels from the belts and dropped them into the designated
boxes. When the customer had made his final purchase he
turned in his traveler and it was sent up to the shipping room,
where it was checked against the contents of the appropriately
numbered box. Then the packages were stuffed into a basket and
the customer's order was ready for the delivery truck.

The main conveyor into which all the subsidiary lines fed, and
which brought the packages up from the heart of the market,
was called, quite improperly, the "chute." A true chute operates
downward, not upward. In moments of stress the chute would
sometimes become jammed with a wildly miscellaneous jumble
of groceries. Other parcels would gather behind these, squirm
and twist and dive like distraught pollywogs, and occasionally
leap over the side. The disorder was easily cleared by a couple
of clerks who would mount stepladders and get the unruly
packages back in line. Any impending chaos was likely to be
detected first by the youth at the head of the chute in the shipping room, since he was in an ideal position to observe it. A
little Scotsman was frequently assigned to this post, and in the
event of a stoppage he would work himself up into a frenzy of
executiveness.

"Chüte is stuck! Chüte is stuck!" he would shriek, umlauts
and all, and dance up and down with generalship. Then, sure
enough, the two clerks would appear on the stepladders—at his
bidding, by his orders, to obey his implied behest—and clear the
channel. For the rest of that day the fellow would fairly drip
complacency and self-importance.

I cannot say that sorting packages in the shipping room was
altogether my conception of the earthly paradise, but it was

much more diverting than working on the poultry counter, a job to which Mr. Senior or Mr. Sutherland assigned me far oftener than met with my approval. My duties here consisted in taking chickens, ducks, geese, and turkeys—particularly turkeys —out to the cutting room to be cleaned.

A dozen or so butchers were employed in the cutting room. Ordinarily their work was dull and routine enough, but there were two processes which I used to watch with unalloyed fascination. These were the larding of a tenderloin of beef and the construction of a crown roast of lamb. The beef-larder would take a stout steel needle with a hollow end about a quarter-inch in diameter, insert a strip of fat salt pork perhaps three inches long into the hollow, stick the sharp end of the needle into the beef, push and pull it through, and detach the strip from the needle as it emerged. The strips were spaced about an inch apart in every direction, and little bits of them were left sticking out on both sides of the tenderloin. One's mouth watered at watching this superb act of creation. As for the butcher himself, I marveled that he did not dash out of the place with a yell, his masterpiece under his arm, in search of the nearest oven.

The crown roast did not seem likely, in my view, to prove nearly so succulent a morsel as the larded tenderloin, but its consummation was even more of an artistic achievement. The butcher would take a length of rib lamb chops, chip and carve it daintily, bend it back into a circle, and skewer the ends together. The result was as lovely a diadem as ever graced Titania's brow. The crown roast was packed for shipment in a special box, and for all I know was delivered under police escort. Mr. Swanson seemed to be particularly enamored of crown roasts, for every second or third Saturday one would leave the cutting room with his name on the box.

By comparison with these artists, the poultry cleaners were the merest pick-and-shovel men. Every time I took a batch of tur-

August drew out a piece of paper and a tiny snapshot.

keys out to the cutting room I would drop them on a table near one of the cleaners and take back any that were already cleaned. These I would wrap individually in great swaths of paper and deliver to waiting customers or toss on the shipping-room belt. There is a special technique to wrapping a turkey, but once he has acquired this a turkey-wrapper can function satisfactorily even in his sleep. I know. After two strenuous sixteen-hour pre-Thanksgiving days at Providence Public Market I once tottered to bed only to awaken an hour later in chill and undraped darkness. I felt around for the bedclothes and could not find them. I turned on the light. The bedclothes were in a neat turkey-package at the foot of the bed.

Most of the turkeys with which I did business came from upstate New York—an area into which I had not up to that time penetrated but with much of which I felt a scholastic kinship. I was studying Latin and Greek at Classical High School, and so was familiar with the names of Utica, Syracuse, Rome, Troy, Ithaca, and Seneca Falls, though I had never up to that time heard of Athens, Attica, Romulus, Cincinnatus, Fabius, Tully, Macedon, Cato, Camillus, Marcellus, Marathon, Carthage, Corinth, Palatine Bridge, Minerva, Niobe, Damascus, Euclid, Plato, Pompey, Hannibal, Hector, Homer, or Virgil.

I knew the turkeys came from upstate New York for this reason: Most people who bought poultry wanted it cleaned in the market, and they usually wanted to salvage the edible organs. To birds ordered by such people, I attached a notice which read "Save the giblets." The cleaner in the cutting room would slit the fowl, thrust in a hand, and extract the unpleasant insides. Occasionally he would pull out with these a gory scrap of paper, hidden there by a romantic, or perhaps merely frivolous, young woman, reading, "Please write Mary So-and-So," or "I would like to hear from you. Anna Such-a-One," with an address appended—usually a town in upstate New York.

The insertion of such a missive involved cutting a tiny slit in the turkey's belly, a procedure of no great benefit to the turkey, but I can say that none of the turkeys I saw ever showed the slightest ill effects from the operation. In every instance, it appeared to have been performed with almost surgical skill—undoubtedly while the boss was not looking.

The cleaners with whom I had most traffic were Carl and August. Both had been born in Germany—at about the same time, I guessed, but Carl had certainly come to this country several years ahead of August. Though Carl's English had traces of a German accent, it was thoroughly idiomatic and understandable. He called August "Aw-gust," to show that he knew better than to call him "Owgoost." August's accent was far more noticeable than Carl's, and his English was subject to lapses, distortions, and confusions. He obviously thought in German and translated into English, and found both processes difficult. Like many stupid people, he was excessively good-natured.

Carl was inclined to be irritable and sarcastic. He patronized August unmercifully, but August, if he assumed anything, probably assumed that this was only the custom of the country and that he had come over too late in life ever to acquire such fine manners.

One Saturday morning I stood watching August excavate, with plodding deftness, the viscera from a fine twenty-two-pound bird. As his hand emerged, I saw that it held a tightly rolled, smeared, payroll-size envelope. August wiped his fingers on his apron, unrolled the envelope, and studied it. It was inscribed "To Whom It May Concern."

"What means?" August asked me. " 'Concern.' Ziss market? Ziss concern?"

"No, it means anybody—whoever gets it," I said.

"Funny way to mean anybody," August said.

"It's used on references. When you go after a new job and don't know who you're going to see."

"Don't let that worry you, Aw-gust," said Carl. "Nobody ain't never goin' to give you no references."

August tore the envelope open and drew out a piece of paper and a tiny snapshot. He inspected the snapshot intently.

"Pooty *good,* pooty *good,*" he said.

Carl and I stood alongside him, right and left, and looked at the photograph. It was of a buxom, flaxen-haired young woman in a low-cut middy blouse. She had good teeth and an insipid mouth. Insipidity meant nothing to August.

"Pooty *damn* good!"

"What you mean 'pooty damn good'?" Carl asked. "If I ever see a come-on smile, that chippie's got it."

"What means 'come-on smile'?"

"Man-hungry, that's what she is," Carl explained. "Anything in pants. Even you, Aw-gust. What's the letter say?"

August unfolded it, blinked, and then handed it to me. "You read," he said.

I read. It said, in a microscopic hand, that Irma Matzheimer (to give her a name) would be happy to correspond with any gentleman who found the note and photograph. Irma described her appearance explicitly. She had been born in Germany and had come here with her family when she was a baby. The return address was R.F.D. Ilion, New York.

"That's the old name for Troy!" I explained with delight.

"Troy?" said Carl. "That's where they make collars. What's Troy got to do with this other place?"

"Is called what, this city?" asked August, before I could embark on an exegesis on classical nomenclature.

"Ilion," I said.

"Write, please, in printing letters," August said.

I printed ILION.

"Ah, I see!" August exclaimed. "I lion."

He said it just like that—I plus lion.

"*Il*ion," I said.

"I lion or I lion—what difference does it matter?" August said.

I went into considerable detail, and got nowhere. It became plain, after ten minutes during which I made two or three turkey-toting trips to and from the poultry counter, that when August said "I lion," he thought he was saying "*Il*ion."

"They ain't nobody so dumb as a dumb Dutchman," Carl said with resignation.

"I bet you maybe Irma don't think so, too," August said, grinning.

"Gawd, awready it's Irma," Carl said. "Irma from Ilion."

"Good!" approved August. "Very *damn* good! Irma from I lion!"

On his way to lunch, August stopped at the poultry counter and beckoned me. "You make for me an answer, please?" he asked. "Carl says you can do it good."

"What do you want to say?"

"About me," August said, "I am five feet ten inch. I am hunnerd ninety-seven pound. I am collar sixteen and half, shoe ten D."

"Why do you have to say all that?" I asked. "Well, all right, if you want to. Let me put down those figures. I'll write the answer tomorrow and bring it in Monday after school. And haven't you got a picture?"

"Sure I got pitcher," August said. "*Good* one. I bring Monday. You bring letter. Good boy!"

I devoted much of Sunday afternoon to drafting the letter. I had neglected to ask August just how far I was to go. Should it be an out-and-out proposal—the direct frontal attack? Or should I adopt the suave approach—a sort of jockeying for position? I decided on the latter. After all, August and Irma should know a little more about each other. Scraps of useful information might emerge—hereditary insanity, a tendency to kleptomania, congenital deafness, two thousand dollars in the bank. I composed a friendly, factual, carefully conservative message.

On Monday afternoon I showed it to August. He was pleased.

"Good! Very good! Very *damn* good!" he exclaimed. "Is one mistake—I make it, not you. Should be shoe eleven D. You change it, please."

"What do you want to change it for?" Carl asked. "The kid writes you a nice, clean letter and you want him to dirty it all up because you don't know how big is your own feet. Let it go ten D. You think this Irma's goin' to like you or hate you just for one size difference in your shoes? The hell with it!"

Both August and I agreed, somewhat hesitantly, to this piece of deception. I gave August my fountain pen and he signed the letter with a spidery and splattery flourish. It took him quite a while. The signature was as impressive as it was indecipherable, but I had had the foresight to begin his letter with "My name is" and "My address is," so no harm was done.

"How about the picture?" I asked.

"I got," said August, and went over to his locker. He returned with a large mounted photograph, about twelve by fifteen inches, of what might have been the entire population of a thriving Bavarian hamlet. August himself, in a tightly fitting black suit and wearing a noble mustache which had subsequently been shaved off, occupied a moderately conspicuous position toward the left of the assembly. "My family," he explained proudly.

"Holy smoke!" Carl said. "You want to scare the girl to death? You want her to think she's adoptin' all them immigrant Dutchmen?"

August held up a mollifying finger. "Under here," he said, indicating his own likeness, "I write 'me.'"

"Hell of a lot of good that will do," Carl said. "She sees that crowd before she sees any 'me' business and awready it's too late. You want to cook your own goose, you just send that pitcher."

"Why don't you get a tintype of yourself out at Roger Williams Park?" I suggested. "I know the man who makes them—his name is Percy White. You could go out Sunday. I'll write at the bottom of the letter, 'Photo will follow,' and that will give her something to look forward to. We can send the letter anyway."

"That's an idea," Carl said. "Get that letter mailed quick, Awgust. Gawd knows how many turkeys got Irma's letters inside of 'em. And look, kid," he added to me, "you better mail that letter yourself. This Dutchman ain't been in this country long enough to tell a letter box from a firebox."

"Is one red and one green," August said.

"Yeah? Which one is which?" Carl asked.

August disdained to reply, but winked at me with calm assurance.

On Sunday he presented himself at Percy White's little studio in Roger Williams Park, and on Monday I went to the Public Market to see the result. Mr. White knew his trade. He had managed to pose August with a certain degree of casualness and had even given him an air of pleased anticipation, as if he had just ordered a seidel of Münchner.

"Honest to Gawd, Aw-gust, that's swell!" Carl said. "You really look like you got some brains in your dumb head."

"I got brains by the galore," August said. "Look, maybe I tell you something sometime you believe it."

"Sure, sometime, maybe. On'y not this time."

The tintype was mailed without accompanying documentation, save for "Sincerely your friend" in my hand on the pink flap that protected the surface, followed by August's own signature.

When I came in to work the following Friday afternoon, I learned that August had had an answer only that morning. Irma had received both letter and tintype and was much impressed. She had looked up Providence on the map. It didn't seem so awfully far from Ilion. Couldn't August come up for a visit? Her mother would make up a special batch of *Sauerbraten* and *Pfannkuchen*.

"Means she can't cook by herself," Carl said. "The old lady has to do it. Watch yourself, Aw-gust."

Irma also explained that her father conducted a prosperous poultry establishment and that they lived in a big house with plenty of room in it, since her two brothers had gone out West together on some joint venture a few months earlier.

"The old man needs a hired hand," Carl said. "Aw-gust should have to do the work of them two Dutchmen, and I bet you they was big huskies, too, on'y they wouldn't stand for no slave-drivin'."

"How you know all that?" August asked. "Where says she that, please?"

"Oh, she wouldn't say it, Aw-gust. You just got to read it inside the lines. If you owed Carnegie a million dollars, would you go tell everybody?"

While August struggled with this devastating hypothetical situation, I read the rest of the letter. It was written in an unformed, schoolgirlish hand and filled with little details of life on the Matzheimer farm—a life that appeared to be of the pleasantest and most idyllic sort. While the letter nowhere overstepped the bounds of propriety or employed even a remotely amatory phrase, it managed to imply that if Irma were sitting in the middle of a sofa and August came into the room, she would immediately move over and make a place for him.

I started to put the letter back into the envelope when I saw a scrap of writing under the flap. "August, August!" I cried. "Did you see this?"

August peered at the writing, and his lips moved as he read it. Then he smacked them, and then put the flap to them.

"For Gawd's sake, is he crazy?" Carl asked.

"Crazy? Ha-ha! Sure am I crazy! Look, you can read, maybe. No, I read to you. It says, 'Ziss is a kiss from Irma to August'!"

"Looks like Providence Public Market is going to hire a new chicken-gutter," Carl said sadly. "Don't bring him no more birds today. He'll go bustin' all the gall bladders and give the place a bad name."

August did indeed tread air and hum little German melodies right up to eleven o'clock Saturday night. By the following Friday he was gone. It was several months before we heard from him. Then, one day, I received a scrawled postal card which, when transliterated and reduced to less involute English, read something like this: "Met nice German widow here who runs little bakery. Doing nice business. We got married two weeks ago today. Railroad sold me wrong ticket and I did not go to other place." The postmark was Lyons, New York.

VIII

Pussy's in the Well

DURING the summer vacation between my junior and
senior years in high school I worked as a delivery boy
for the George W. Dover Company of Providence,
manufacturers of jewelers' findings. At that time Providence was
the jewelry capital of America. I suppose it still is.

Jewelers' findings were the doodads which manufacturing
jewelers converted into belt buckles, shoe buckles, stickpins, hat-
pins, lockets, watch fobs, cuff links, brooches. The favorite sub-
jects of that period—it was 1907—were fleurs-de-lis, daisies,
hearts, Moors' heads (full face), dogs' and horses' and Indians'
heads (profile), and, above all, swastikas. Adolf Hitler was only
eighteen years old at the moment and had probably never heard
of the swastika, which is about as German as chow mein.

The Dover Company daily stamped out thousands of these
devices, which were taken to the stock room and stored against
orders. Every morning I filled a great canvas satchel with
packages of made-up orders and took them to the dozens of
manufacturing jewelers' shops, big and little, which were
crowded into the neighborhood.

There was no Mr. Dover in the Dover Company at that time.
Our top chiefs were Mr. Mays, Mr. Stone, and Mr. Briggs—a
pleasant trio who got on well with each other and with every-
body else. Mr. Stone had been a classmate of John D. Rockefeller,
Jr., at Brown University, and had probably once called Mr.
Rockefeller John, or, at worst, plain Rockefeller. My imme-

64

diate boss, the head of the stock-room, was named Morris, but I have no idea at this date whether that was his first or last name.

This was my first steady, all-day, week-after-week job (at four dollars a week)—the first hint I ever had of what permanent employment would be like. I did not mind working all summer, but I should have preferred something other than delivering jewelers' findings. My ambition had always been—I can almost say has always been—to be a bellboy in a summer hotel in the White Mountains. I never attained this proud goal. One reason for the failure may be that I never wrote to any summer hotel to ask if they wanted me.

My delivery route lay close to the Providence water front—a locality which, while not altogether so romantic a spot as it had been in the old days of ginseng, molasses and rum, was nevertheless authentically maritime. Whenever I had a lean morning, or had been unusually zealous in the performance of my duties, I would return to the office by way of the wharves, pausing occasionally to watch a coal barge or a lumber schooner discharge its cargo.

It was on one of these pleasant and mildly illicit excursions that I met Mickey. The fact that each of us carried a large canvas bag made introductions inevitable. Mickey worked for another findings house, but we did not regard the competitive spirit as reaching down as far as ourselves. Mickey was slight, wiry, sandy-haired, freckled, and a year or two younger than I. He could spit at a forty-five-degree angle, thanks to a missing canine tooth on the left side. Since he was a frequent and unpredictable spitter, it was the part of discretion to walk on his right.

Mickey and I would frequently meet a policeman named Tim, who was always glad to pass the time of day or to join in any discussion in which Mickey and I might have become involved. Mickey was a persistent seeker after knowledge concerning anything under the sun, and since I was willing to risk a guess about anything I didn't know, his head must have contained a queer medley of truth and error. In case he questioned the accuracy or validity of any of my statements (which he did not do often enough, and more often when I was right than when I was wrong), he would turn the matter over to Tim for resolution. Mickey accepted Tim's authority completely. I could not go quite so far as that, but it seemed wise to suppress any doubts I might have regarding Tim's omniscience.

One morning when we were watching an excursion steamer, probably the *Mount Hope,* loading passengers for a trip down the bay to Newport, I mentioned the fact that Newport had once been the second capital of Rhode Island.

"Wait a minute," said Mickey. "You mean Providence and Newport was both capitals?"

"That's right."

"Oh, go on! What would a little state like Rhode Island want with two capitals?"

"I don't know—it just had them."

"That's a crazy idea. Look how big Massachusetts is and they on'y got Boston. And how about Texas—they on'y got one capital, ain't they?"

Every Providence schoolboy was and is and always will be aware and proud of the fact that Rhode Island is one two-hundred-and-twentieth as big as Texas.

I admitted that Texas was as deficient in capitals as Mickey had surmised.

"Well, gee, if we had two capitals here once, then Texas should ought to had hundreds. Look—here comes Tim. Hey, Tim, Newport wasn't never a capital like Providence, was it?"

Tim was probably much more familiar with the political geography of County Mayo than with that of Rhode Island, but his prestige would suffer if he were forced to admit it. The law

Tim broke into a sprint, working his way out of his coat as he ran.

is always right. Moreover, whenever Tim stood in judgment over Mickey and me he was always sure of a two-to-one decision.

"Newport people is too rich to want to rub elbows wit' politicians," he said. "Also they would not like a big capitol building down there, dome and all, because it would make some of thim marble palaces they got look like nothing."

I noticed that Tim had slid around the question at issue, but I held my peace. Mickey pranced in triumph and swung his canvas satchel around until it was difficult to say whether he was swinging the satchel or the satchel him. We walked along with Tim until Mickey and I decided it was time we returned to our shops.

On another occasion Mickey and I became involved in a discussion of the indestructibility of matter. We had been watching an orange crate burn in a gutter, and I had attempted to explain that the consumed material had turned into various kinds of gases, but that everything in the crate was still in existence.

"But you couldn't put oranges in that crate still, could you?"

"No, I didn't say—"

"Then what good is it?"

"I didn't say it was *any* good. I just said everything in it was still somewhere."

"All right—everything in it is somewhere. Your old man smokes cigars, maybe."

I said he did occasionally.

"All right—supposin' he smokes a cigar and even when he's finished it that cigar is still a cigar, now what does that do to the cigar business? Supposin' your old man was in the cigar business, huh? How you gonna eat?"

"I didn't say—"

"Why do we have fire engines, like the Three Ones over on Exchange Place? Supposin' a house catches fire, you just let it burn, huh? It ain't really burnt at all—it's still there. On'y I bet if your old man owned it he'd be mad as hell just the same. Hey, Tim,"—our referee rounded a corner—"hey, Tim, do you smoke cigars?"

"Why, now, Mickey, thank ye, from time to time I do that."

"Tim, I don't mean I got a cigar—I ain't got a cigar—but I mean you could on'y smoke one cigar once, couldn't you?"

"On'y one cigar once," mused Tim. "You mean smoke two cigars in my mouth at one time? Like on a bet or something? Or for a joke like?"

"No, no! Lookit—you smoke a cigar, see, and it's all gone, huh? You couldn't smoke that same cigar again, huh?"

"That's not what I told him," I put in. "I mean when you smoke a cigar the tobacco turns into something else—ashes and smoke and different gases."

"Well," said Tim, "I don't know as I can go all the way wit' you on that. Maybe in some cheap cigars, sure, but now you take a real good nickel cigar, there ain't no gas in that. And you talk about ashes and smoke—well, what the hell, a cigar don't do you a damn bit of good until it turns into ashes and smoke, does it? You leave it just like it is and what good is it doing anybody? You smoke it and you're getting your money's worth out of it, ain't you?"

I accepted this, because it at least constituted complete refutation of Mickey's thesis about smoking the same cigar twice.

We did not appeal to Tim's arbitrament every time we met him, because Mickey and I did not become involved in an argument every time we met—in fact, we agreed on more things than we disagreed. It was good to listen to Tim's philosophy and to any details of his experiences that he might vouchsafe us. We pressed him for these daily.

"I would make up a good story for ye if it was allowable to do so," he said to us, "but I have to stick to the trut'. One drunk is just like another, on'y some you got to push and some you got to pull. Now if anything was to really happen on this beat, damn if I don't think I could tell you about it as well as the next one."

It was only a few days after this that I found Mickey sitting on the edge of our favorite wharf, with the murky and malodorous waters of the Providence River a few feet below him. He did not have his canvas satchel with him; instead he was clasping to his stomach a square cardboard box.

"You wouldn't guess what I got here if I was to give you ten million guesses."

I told him that in that case I wouldn't try.

Mickey removed the cover with ceremonious caution. I peered inside and saw what looked like the hide of some unidentifiable fur-bearing creature—a superannuated tomcat, perhaps, for the fur was silvery. On the skin side were three discs, each about the size of a dime, which meant nothing at all to me.

"What is it?"

"My boss's wig," said Mickey in a hoarse, conspiratorial whisper.

"What are those round things for?"

"They put little bits of wax there and his head melts them enough so that the wig sticks. They wear out or sump'n' so every once in a while I have to take it to a wig feller for new ones."

"If he has to wear a wig why does he wear one with old man's hair? Why doesn't he wear a black one or a brown one?"

"He's got a mustache that color so he has to match it, and he's got some little bits of real hair this color around his ears and down his neck. This thing don't make him look so old. He looks a hell of a lot older without it."

"What's he doing right now—going around bald-headed?"

"No, sirree. He has another wig he wears in the shop. This is for dress-up. Let's see how you'd look if you was an old man."

He took the wig out of the box and put it on my head. I stuck out my chin and put my lower lip over my upper to indicate I had no teeth; then I made believe I had a cane and began hobbling about the wharf. Mickey cackled with joy, clapped his hands, stamped his feet. And when I picked up my canvas satchel, flung it over my shoulder, and announced "Santa Claus," I brought down my one-man house.

"Let me do it!" Mickey cried.

He copied my performance and added nuances of his own, including a graphic portrayal of his employer. It was all thoroughly delightful.

"Wonder how I look in it," he said at the end of his act. He went to the edge of the wharf, got down on hands and knees, and leaned over to catch his reflection in the black mirror of the river. The wig fell into the water.

Mickey leaped to his feet with a terrified scream and began prancing up and down and waving his arms like pinwheels. And just then Tim appeared, walking with his slow, dignified patrolman stride. He heard Mickey, saw him pointing frantically down at the water. Tim broke into a sprint, working his way out of his coat as he ran and flinging his helmet aside. He saw the wig, floating hair-side up. Feet first, over and in he went.

It had all taken fractions of seconds, and the dramatic surge of it had left Mickey and me spellbound and inarticulate. Anyway, only a spoilsport would have raised finger or voice to stay that magnificent dash. I doubt, too, whether, once Tim had got his original idea, we should have had time to supplant it with a new one.

Tim came to the surface and struck out for the wig. He grabbed for it in orthodox lifesaving fashion, and contrived a roar of horror and dismay when, as it seemed to him, the victim's scalp came off in his hand.

"Hold onto it!" screamed Mickey. "It's my boss's!"

Meantime the skipper of a coal barge that was tied up at the next wharf had been aroused by the commotion and now stood poised with a life belt which he dropped neatly and flatly at Tim's side. Tim got aboard the barge and disappeared into the skipper's quarters aft. Presently the skipper emerged with Tim's trousers, shirt, socks, and underwear and hung them out on a washline in the bright sun.

"We better take him his coat and helmet," I suggested.

"*You* do it," Mickey pleaded.

"You want your wig, don't you?"

Mickey saw the logic of that. We boarded the barge and timorously opened the cabin door. Tim was drying himself vigorously and talking softly.

"I'm sorry you got wet, Tim," said Mickey.

Tim glared at him for a moment, then threw his head back and laughed so that his naked belly rippled.

"It might be I was in need of a bath," he said, "but that's a hell of a place to pick for it. And I'm tellin' the pair of ye to never say a God-damned word about this or, by all the Holy Saints, I'll knock your blocks off both together. Go on now—take your piece of fuzz and git!"

Parasangs and Molecules

MR. DRAKE was my room teacher in my third year at Classical High School. He had white hair and a white mustache and wore gold-rimmed glasses. He was an admirable instructor and a thorough gentleman. The students liked and respected him and he liked and respected the students. But for whatever reason, most of the hell-raising that went on in Classical High, and that was a lot, occurred in Mr. Drake's room.

It could not have been Mr. Drake's fault. I think now that the explanation is that a high school sophomore does not attain the true heights of sophomoricality in his sophomore year. During his sophomore year he knows that he is, quite literally, a "wise fool." He therefore struggles against being a wise fool as hard as he can. But in his junior year he becomes, without being aware of it, a foolish wise man. In his junior year he needs a good teacher, for by now he is ready and able and eager and willing to learn. But the inhibited hellishness of his second year bursts out of him with a roar. He is like a man of fifty-five at a convention.

It is a tough spot even for a perfect teacher. The third year in high school, I suggest, is like third base in baseball. It is the hot corner. Drake at third. The right man in the right place.

It was while I was in Mr. Drake's room that someone put *two* alarm clocks (practically the whole class had chipped in to buy them) in empty desks, set to go off a quarter of an hour apart.

73

They did. Mr. Drake took both clocks in stride, set them on his desk, said he hadn't realized the class needed *that* much waking up, and went on with the lesson.

It was while I was in Mr. Drake's room that someone put a frightfully foul-smelling mess—reputedly valerianate of ammonia—in one of the empty desks that had concealed the alarm clocks. The room was uninhabitable for a week. (We did not get the week off.) Everybody in the class, including the unidentified perpetrator of the outrage (we hadn't chipped in for *that* one), suffered equally with Mr. Drake.

It was while I was in Mr. Drake's room that I myself was sent home for socking an unsuspecting classmate across the aisle and ordered not to return until a parent had talked things over with Mr. Drake. By pure chance my stepmother had been a Sunday School pupil of Mr. Drake's at Trinity Methodist (obviously Mr. Drake was the complete busman). Mr. Drake got considerable of a jolt when my stepmother went to see him on my behalf. She talked over old times at Trinity and then listened to a recital of my merits and my defects. This took some time. I went back to school next day, and for the rest of the year my deportment was, by and large, admirable. There *was* one incident a few months later, but that incident had nothing to do with deportment as that attribute is interpreted on report cards. To me it is memorable because it elicited from Mr. Drake the greatest compliment that has ever been paid me in all my life—a somewhat backhanded compliment, but the greatest none the less.

Mr. Drake's specialty was Greek. He knew Greek and he knew how to teach it. We had started to learn Greek in our sophomore year, under Mr. Jacobs—also a good teacher, but rougher, tougher, and gruffer than Mr. Drake. Mr. Jacobs had black, parted-in-the-middle hair which kept falling down over his eyes and ears and which he kept shaking back out of the way. He also

Mr. Drake said he hadn't realized the class needed *that* much waking up.

had prominent upper front teeth which he would tap with a pencil while we were reciting. If all was going well he would tap gently and almost inaudibly; if all was not going well he would bang away at himself like a machine gun. Frequently when a pupil faltered Mr. Jacobs would inquire sharply: "Did you look over this Greek?" The answer to that, of course, was yes. "I guess you overlooked it. Sit down."

It was under Mr. Jacobs' tutelage that we were first conducted into Xenophon's *Anabasis*: "*Dareiou kai Parusatidos gignontai paides duo, presbuteros men Artaxerxes, neoteros de Kuros*— Of Darius and Parysatis were born two sons, the elder Artaxerxes, the younger Cyrus. After Darius had fallen sick, and feared that his end was approaching, he wished both of his sons to attend him. The elder happened to be present; Cyrus was sent for from the province of which he was satrap. Cyrus accordingly went up, taking with him Tissaphernes as a friend, and having also with him three hundred heavy-armed Greeks. But when Darius was dead, and Artaxerxes was placed upon the throne, Tissaphernes brought an accusation against Cyrus before his brother, saying that Cyrus was plotting against him. Artaxerxes was induced to believe this, and had Cyrus arrested with the intention of putting him to death, but his mother, having begged his life, sent him back to his province. When Cyrus had departed, after being thus in danger and disgrace, he began to consider by what means he might cease to be subject to his brother, and make himself king, if he could, in his stead."

Recently I looked into a school text of the *Anabasis* to see if I could make anything of it. I found it pretty hard sledding. The Greeks were always coming to a *polis oikomene* (I could remember that)—an "inhabited city," probably a cluster of four or five mud hovels; and they were always on the go—*enteuthen exelaunei parasangas triakonta kai pente*—"thence they marched thirty-five parasangs," not in a day, God help them, not even if they had had Patton's tanks, for a parasang averaged three miles or so (it was a measurement of time rather than of distance). We Greek students got to measuring distances around Providence in parasangs, and somebody evolved a couplet:

> Cyrus marched a parasang
> And then sat down and said "Oh, hang!"

—or something like that.

It was quite a good story, this *Anabasis,* for something you had to read, and had to read in a foreign language. It was much more interesting than Caesar's account of his campaigns in Gaul, the main difference being that Caesar wrote a report and Xenophon was a reporter. Caesar, moreover, had everything his own way— he came, he saw, he conquered. The Greeks came, saw, and took it on the chin. Cyrus assembled an army of around a hundred thousand Persians and also hired some fourteen thousand Greeks who had been fighting in the Peloponnesian War and knew no other trade. Casualties and desertions reduced the total to ten thousand. Artaxerxes collected a force of nine hundred thousand—a whopping big army for 401 B.C.—and marched against Cyrus. They met on the east bank of the Euphrates at Cunaxa. Cyrus was killed. The Greeks had done pretty well on their bit of front, but winning a single smart tactical success was not winning a war. There they were, outnumbered nearly a hundred to one, stripped of all supplies save for such K-rations as they had tucked in their belts, nearly fifteen hundred miles from home, with a desolate, hostile, mountainous country in between, and winter coming on. They made it, some of them, and five months later, around Lincoln's birthday, they reached the shores of the Black Sea. Xenophon's account of that great moment climaxes one of the most dramatic eyewitness recitals in history:

When the men who were in the front had mounted the height, and looked upon the sea, a great shouting proceeded from them; and Xenophon and the rear guard, on hearing it, thought that some new enemies were assailing the front, for in the rear, too, the people from the country that they had burned were following them, and the rear guard, by placing an ambuscade, had killed some, and made others prisoner, and had captured about twenty shields made of raw oxhide with the hair on. But as the noise still increased, and drew nearer, and as those who came up from time to time kept running at full speed to join those who were continually shouting, the cries becoming louder as the men became more numerous, it appeared to Xenophon that it must be something of great moment. Mounting his horse, therefore, and taking with him Lycius and the cavalry, he hastened forward to give aid, when presently they heard the soldiers shouting "The sea, the sea!" and cheering on one another. Then they all began to run, the rear guard as well as the rest, and the baggage cattle and horses were put to their speed; and when they had all arrived at the top, the men embraced one another, and their generals and captains, with tears in their eyes.

In our sophomore year, while we were still in Mr. Jacobs' room, we had also studied physics under Mr. Berry, who was a sound instructor but very severe. He would mark a student down for a stupid question as quickly as he would for a stupid answer. This trap once snapped on me when I asked what the numerals on a barometer stood for. In spite of this lapse, when we reached our junior year and abandoned physics (forever, so far as I was concerned) in favor of chemistry, Mr. Berry asked me if I would like to work for him after school hours—preparing apparatus, mixing solutions, and so on. He would pay me twenty cents an hour.

I accepted the offer on the spot. The road to riches did not lie that way, to be sure, because Mr. Berry made it clear that three hours would be a big week's work. But the work would be novel and pleasant, and sixty cents was sixty cents. At this late date I feel free to confess that I did a little experimenting on my own (and on my own time), and consumed some small part of the laboratory supplies, provided by the city of Providence, in manufacturing tiny specimens of gunpowder and setting these off with a Bunsen burner. For a few weeks I considered becoming a chemist, and I still think I should have made a good one if I could have hired someone to help out with all the mathematical drudgery that would have been involved.

Mr. Berry showed me that the acids we used in our experiments were in such weak solution that they could not have done us any harm unless we had drunk a considerable quantity. In proof of this he unstopped a bottle, moistened the end of his finger with acid, and touched the end of his finger to his tongue. In spite of his assurance, I half expected him to drop dead on the spot. Instead he smacked his lips as if he had downed a good bracer. Thereupon I followed suit and found that of the three staple acids at each worktable (sulphuric, nitric, and hydrochloric), hydrochloric had the pleasantest taste. It was, Mr. Berry explained to me, itself one of the gastric juices, as an occasional eupeptic eructation will prove to anybody. Thereafter I used to startle my schoolfellows in chemistry class by popping an acid-doused fingertip into my mouth and then rubbing my stomach in high contentment and saying, "Ahhhhhh!"

It was not long after I took over the job of being Mr. Berry's assistant that things began settling down to normal in Mr. Drake's room. So far as I personally was concerned, this may have been, in some part, cause and effect. After all, I was now almost a member of the faculty, and it would no longer do to yank Earl Perkins's neat bow tie out of its knot or bop Ted Fletcher over the head with an algebra.

Whenever Mr. Drake called on me to translate a fragment of Xenophon I accommodated with verve and accuracy. Mr. Drake would then set down a mark in a little book. That little book indicated not only how well or how poorly each of us was doing, but also how often we were called upon to perform. Each of us appeared to average roughly one recitation every three days. Mr. Drake probably had some little system about that—nothing hard and fast, nothing we could catch onto, but a system none the less.

There came a time, however, when the system seemed to go completely askew. I was called on for three days in a row. On each occasion I got myself and the retreating Greeks out of our respective difficulties and was certain that Mr. Drake had put a 9 alongside my name in his little book.

The evening after my third successive recitation I did not even bother to open my Xenophon. Instead I read a G. A. Henty book and played clock solitaire. It was good to have a night off. Next day in Greek class I listened attentively to find out what the *Anabasis* sounded like when one came to a part of it with which one was thoroughly unfamiliar. My classmates certainly made a hash of it. They were halting in their speech and leaned heavily on *er*'s. Didn't the stuff mean anything to them? Didn't they appreciate the jam the Greeks were in? This wasn't just a lesson—it was a story, a true story, a story that G. A. Henty could have done something with. Perhaps he *had* done something with it. I must find out. "With Xenophon in Mesopotamia," or Cappadocia, or Armenia, or—

Incredibly, my name was called. I stood up. I knew the place, but that was about all I did know. I could make out those useless old twins *men* and *de,* but these were merely the Greek equivalents of *ho* and *hum,* so we never bothered to translate them. Xenophon had got the Ten Thousand into strange country, and they were not only doing strange and incomprehensible things, but speaking a strange language. I stumbled, fumbled, guessed, and guessed wrong. Out at third—Drake, unassisted.

"Sit down," said Mr. Drake, making a mark in his little book. "How are the mighty fallen."

X

The Incomplete Arsonist

IF I have any awareness of the intricacies wrapped up in McCulloch *vs.* Maryland or some slight capacity to read *The Canterbury Tales* in a heavily accented Middle English, the credit therefore belongs to the Providence Gas Company. For if it had not been for the Providence Gas Company, I could not have had a college education.

I went with the company just before I entered my second year at Brown University, in September, 1909, and I stayed with the company (or the company with me) until a couple of weeks before my graduation in June, 1912.

Today, I believe, in most cities meters are read by full-time professionals. In my youth, and in Providence, the job was entrusted to zealous amateurs, most of them college students. An eager band of these would report to the gas company's Mr. Wilcox at eight o'clock of a specified morning each month, obtain books, flashlights, and caps, and scatter to their respective districts.

The gilt-lettered "PROV GAS CO" cap which the company supplied each of us was our closest approach to being in uniform, but, thus accoutred, a meter reader was just about as completely in uniform as if he had worn gold braid, sash, epaulettes, and sword. The cap was a Civil War model (may, for all I know, have been Civil War surplus), with a leather visor and a pancake top. Whenever I ducked up the hill between cellars, to attend a class at Brown, I was hailed variously about the campus as

U. S. Grant, the Drummer Boy of Shiloh, or Custer's Last Stand.

Incidentally, the time taken out of a meter-reading day to attend classes was not company time. We were paid by the meter. The figure ranged, as I recall, from one cent to a cent and a fifth, depending on the part of town you were assigned. My book paid a cent and a fifth. My area was a grimy, congested, dismal district which apparently ate and drank illuminating gas. In tenement after tenement there was row upon row of meters—as many as twenty, I remember, in one foul cavern that was my Comstock Lode. On my best day, with no college classes and no halt for lunch, I read five hundred and one meters and earned six dollars and one cent, which was as much as some of my professors were making. I believe this established a sort of record, but I hate to come right out and claim it lest I arouse the competitive spirit of some broken-down old meter-reading master, and there might be a lot of acrimonious give-and-take, with neither one of us being able to prove anything.

A meter reader rarely made (or makes) a mistake. There is no more excuse for reading a meter wrong than for reading a clock wrong. The trick is to read from right to left and write from left to right. "Eight, nine-eight, O-nine-eight," I would say to myself, rotating my flashlight from dial to dial, first clockwise, then counterclockwise, then clockwise again, and I would put down 098. If the previous reading (which I did not have) had been 059, the consumer had burned up three thousand, nine hundred cubic feet of gas in the interval. Nowadays, when a suburban friend who owns a gas heater takes me into the cellar to show me his rowdy bar decorations, I instinctively sidle over to the meter to see if the old eye has lost its cunning. It hasn't.

We meter readers operated under a pretty loose charter. It went without saying that we were expected to be accurate. It also went without saying, or anyhow we readers assumed it did, that if occasionally we had difficulty in getting into a place it would be all right to exercise a certain amount of individual initiative. If a reader had kicked in a door to get at a meter, there would probably have been words about that, but we never informed Mr. Wilcox when it was necessary (as it frequently was) to pick a cheap padlock with a piece of wire.

There was one regulation, however, in which we were schooled with clarity and vigor. On no account were we to tamper with the meter or with the pipes that spiderwebbed out of it. We were workers of the head, not of the hand. To read the meter it was not necessary to touch it or any of its appurtenances. If a consumer reported a leak or other mechanical defect to us it was our duty to inform the office, giving some hint, if we could, of how serious the trouble was. I have, therefore, no excuse to offer for what follows, and I tell it at all only as a warning to others lest they, like me, should think they know everything.

Late one afternoon I started down the cellar entrance of a two-family house whose occupants were a rung or two higher up the economic ladder than the tenants of the warrens in my beat on Constitution Hill. There was never anything furtive about a meter reader. His approach to premises was always forthright and noisy—for two purposes. If there were a dog on the place the dog would begin barking, and the reader, forewarned, would take a firmer grip on his flashlight. Moreover, an honest, manly footstep tended to reassure the householder, and the reader was usually allowed to go about his business undisturbed. Occasionally a nervous housewife would call, "Who is it?" down the cellar stairs, but the reply "Gas man" usually set her fears at rest. Only the ultrasuspicious, the ultrabold, and the ultratimid actually came down cellar for visual confirmation.

This particular house was occupied by a who-is-iter. I said,

The trick is to read from right to left and to write from left to right.

"Gas man," and then footsteps sounded on the cellar stairs. Ah, a come-downer as well. A pair of wrinkled, scuffed high shoes came into view, followed by an apron, an ample and shawled bosom, a compressed mouth, and a pair of belligerent beady little eyes.

"That meter's leakin', and don't you try to tell me it ain't."

There *was* a hint of gas in the air, but nothing to get excited about.

"Don't you tell me it ain't leakin'," repeated the client, before I could contrive a soft answer, "because I know it is. And I know jest where it's leakin', too." She gleefully put a finger on a pin-point hole in one of the pipes. "You jest tetch a match to that and see."

Touching a match to "that" was the one thing the Providence Gas Company, the Providence Fire Department, and the Goddess of Reason and Enlightenment, had they been hovering in the background, would have implored me not to do.

"Did *you* touch a match to it?" I asked.

"Sure," she said, and chuckled. "It lit."

"That is the sort of thing," I said severely, "which should be left to experts."

"Well, you're an expert, ain't you?"

Thus challenged, I touched a lighted match to the speck. It lit. I rubbed a finger over the infinitesimal blue flame and it vanished. I lit it again and rubbed it out again.

"That's nothing to worry about," I said. "I'll report it when I get back to the office half an hour from now." And I did.

That was my last day of reading for the month. The following day I became a full-time student again. That afternoon, to my surprise (and, I may add, to my gratification), I received a telephone call from the gas company. Would I see Mr. Wilcox as soon as possible? Nothing but good, I was convinced, could come of this interview. Perhaps Mr. Wilcox was going to offer me some sort of supervisory position or promote me to a Golconda where there were two-cent meters.

Mr. Wilcox was an austere gentleman who wore a white vest and a perpetual frown. The frown was simply a physical characteristic, for I never knew him to raise his voice or get worked up. I presented myself at his desk.

"Did you read a meter at such-and-such an address yesterday?" he asked.

"Yes, sir."

"Did you test the pipe with a match?"

"Yes, sir." In my mind's ear I heard a flutter of wings. It was the supervisory position flying out of the window, closely followed by my job as a plain meter reader.

"After you left," Mr. Wilcox continued, with calm relentlessness, "they had a fire. They had to call out the department."

My first reaction to this news was a throb of disappointment that I had missed seeing the consummation of my handiwork. For an instant I knew just how Nero had felt, and I envied and sympathized with him. But I pushed these unworthy emotions aside and sprang to my own defense. For I saw I was going to need the best defense I could devise.

I had a good one, I thought. A generation later, I still think so. I told Mr. Wilcox I was positive the leak I had tested was in an iron pipe. Iron conducted the gas in from the main to the neighborhood of the meter, where, because the pipe had to be bent at various places, lead took over. A leak in the iron pipe, tested with a match, would, if left alone, keep on burning forever without increasing in size. But a similar test in a lead pipe would quickly melt the lead and produce a hole through which the flaming gas would pour as from a blowtorch. I also told Mr. Wilcox I was sure I had extinguished the flame, and that it was my opinion that the tenant had subsequently done a little experimenting on her own account, probably detecting a leak in a lead pipe and having a go at that.

Mr. Wilcox listened silently and solemnly. Then he said, "I see," and that closed the examination. I ought, of course, to have been fired on the spot. But I soon realized that by doing nothing at all about the incident, Mr. Wilcox had assured himself of having one meter reader who in future would as soon stick a rattlesnake in his mouth as put a match, or even a finger, to a gas pipe.

I spent much of the next three weeks or so speculating about what might happen when I made my next call at the house where the fire had been. I planned to stake everything on a swift and silent entry and departure. The moment came. I was a little startled, and vastly pleased, to discover not only that the house was still intact but that it showed no exterior sign of damage. Mr. Wilcox had given me no hint of the extent of the catastrophe and it had not seemed advisable to ask.

I sneaked tiptoe down the cellar stairs. Yes, there had been a fire. The rafters were smudged and blackened, but they had been toasted rather than burned, and they were still sturdy. There were streaks of soot on the stone foundation. The floor was too clean—evidently a quantity of debris had been swept up and carried away. In two or three places glistening new boards had, presumably, replaced charred predecessors. It had hardly been a major disaster, but it had certainly been a fire.

I took the meter reading quickly and started stealthily back toward the stairs. Excess of caution made me clumsy, and I upset an axe stuck in a chopping block. It fell to the cement floor with a resonant clang. There were hurried footsteps overhead and a door opened.

"Who is it?" a woman's voice asked.

I was caught like a bug in a bottle. The two cellar windows were shut tight—perhaps nailed tight—and protected outside by heavy wire screening. Moreover, there was probably a law against breaking and exiting, and I was in no mood for fresh crime.

"Who *is* it?" the voice asked again.

"Gas man." I got it out in what was meant to be a rumbling, corner-of-the-mouth bass. I tilted my cap forward and over one ear, so that I must have resembled one of the more raffish members of the old Fifth Wisconsin, and again started toward the stairs.

"You be careful, you gas man. Feller was here last month set the house afire."

The door banged. I walked out a free man. But don't tell me that that woman didn't have a guilty conscience. It is a sure sign of one when somebody is afraid to face somebody else.

XI

Nose-Count

D
URING the spring of every year ending in zero the
United States tots up its people. This procedure is
known, reasonably enough, as the decennial census.
Thousands of enumerators go up and down the land collecting
statistics—not only how many inhabitants but how old, of which
sex, whether citizens or aliens, means of livelihood, owners or
renters of homes, and much more.

Enumerators are chosen—they were, at any rate, in my day—
on the basis of an examination in which applicants fill out sample schedules of the sort which the successful competitors will
use in the actual enumeration. I have always been a demon at
filling out blanks provided no arithmetic is involved, and I had
no difficulty in making the grade when I applied for a job as
enumerator for the 1910 census in Providence.

I was assigned a district which included our own home on
Plainfield Street. Many of the residents of this area worked in
the Olneyville textile mills; among the rest dozens of other call-
ings were represented, most of them in the sweat-of-the-brow
classifications. There were no bank presidents, college professors, artists, editors. There were few doctors, lawyers, clergy-
men. There were plenty of machinists, spinners, motormen,
retail-store salesmen, carpenters, masons, day laborers, school-
teachers, plasterers, molders, and proprietors of small shops.

It took me about two weeks to canvass my district, and I was
able to complete the job without any interference with my col-

lege classes. Payment was two-and-a-half cents an individual. Horses were ten cents—not, unfortunately, each. One horse on the premises or one hundred made no difference. The enumerator merely set down the total number. An ice company had a stable with twenty-five horses—ten cents. My father had Selim —ten cents. We were four persons—ten cents. Good old Selim.

The job of census taking was not without its educational value. I learned quite a bit about human nature, than which there is nothing more natural. I recall no instance of a blanket refusal to answer questions, and only an occasional, readily overcome reluctance to answer some specific question. Many people whose homes were mortgaged (few homes in my district were owned outright, and few enough in any degree) seemed to feel that some sort of disgrace was implied in the fact—a housewife would often say, "Do I *have* to tell you that?"

I learned that if a person could read and write readily—if he had had at least a few grades of elementary school—he would declare that ability with a simple affirmation. If he could barely read and write he would accent his affirmation strongly—"Why, certainly!"—as if that much might surely be taken for granted, and that I had my nerve with me in asking. If he could not read and write he would declare his inability as quickly and unselfconsciously and unemotionally as if he were telling me the color of his eyes. I was astonished, incidentally, at the number of illiterates among my neighbors, and even more at the number of half-literates—people who could read but not write. Having gone so far, one would have thought they might have troubled to go the rest of the way. What had kept them back? Was some redoubtable mental hazard implicit in the act of putting pen or pencil to paper? Did reading, in general, signify pleasure; and writing merely a chore?

I learned that, contrary to the American credo (contrary, indeed, to the universal credo), women were not reluctant to tell their ages. I was no judge of women's ages then, nor am I now—when a newspaper displays the likenesses of Mrs. J. Catesby Appledore and daughter Ethelyn I have to read the left-to-right to find out which is which—and it is quite possible that an occasional understatement was thereby permitted to insinuate itself into the government files, but the answer almost always appeared to be given too quickly and too readily to allow for any mathematical manipulation. True, these were women who in most instances had never seen me before and would probably never see me again—women, moreover, to whom I was a mere official abstraction, but were they stopping to take all that into account as I sat at their kitchen tables with pencil poised to record their answers? I cannot think so.

I did, naturally, feel some embarrassment in interviewing people I knew. I had the sensation of poking about in their desk drawers, opening their mail, peering over their shoulders as they read it. In these cases I tried to appear wholly detached and official, but it was quite a strain all around, and I got the business over with as quickly as possible, and went.

There was one category in which some slight afflatus of the ego was often attempted, almost always by a man, or by a wife on her husband's behalf—in that era the men were winning most of the bread, though there were plenty of girls in the textile mills. Everyone, it seems, wants to make his job sound a little more important than it is. I recall no one who said right out that he was a ditchdigger or a street sweeper—he "worked for Jones and Smith, the contractors," or "for the City." Yes, but just what did he do? It often took some probing to get the answer. "He's a clerk in a drugstore" was frequently refined down to the fact that "he" was a soda-jerker, or, more elegantly, a soda-dispenser. "Clerk," "salesman" and "agent" were the bane of every enumerator's existence.

I had no adventures, was involved in no incidents, during my

The job of census taking was not without its educational value.

brief census-taking career. Looking back, I see myself for
exactly what I was—an assembler of impersonal statistics. Out
of the five hundred or more families I interviewed, only one, outside of my own, survives as a vivid, authentic, flesh-and-blood
recollection.

One afternoon I came to a plain box of a house, painted an
indifferent white, in one of the meaner backwaters of my district. It was two-and-a-half stories high and it might or might
not shelter two families—if it did, they were packed in pretty
snugly. Yes, there were two families—so much the better for
me. I collected the data on the downstairs people and walked up
the bare wooden stairs to the second floor.

A huge, good-natured woman of indeterminate age admitted
me to the kitchen and directed me to a chair. I was struck by the
impeccable neatness of the room. I had seen enough kitchens
during the past few days (I always went to the back door) to be
something of an authority, or at least to be able to make com-
parisons. Nowhere had I seen a brighter, cleaner, more cheerful
room than this. It smelled clean, too. Nowhere could I detect
that fetor of the prolific poor which I had come to know so well
—a blend in which cabbage and unwashed diapers always appeared to predominate. Yet here obviously was a household only
a step or two away from the verge of destitution, the husband
probably a mill hand. Perhaps there were no children, but that
would make it a fantastic exception.

"Your husband's name, please?"

She gave it. It was Irish. As I had guessed, he was a textile
worker.

"Any children?"

"Nine."

I wondered where she put them all. She gave me their names
and ages, beginning with the oldest. The oldest was fourteen,
and therefore old enough to work, and working, in the mill.

Then a routine question, here purely perfunctory:

"Any others in the family?"

"Yes. We adopted my husband's brother's children. Their father and mother are dead."

"How many are there?"

"Six."

"Six, in addition to nine of your own?"

"That's right."

She grinned. Apparently I was not the first to wonder how she managed. I haven't given up wondering.

The little nieces and nephews were all too young to work. She gave me the data on them. Seventeen persons. Forty-two and a half cents for me. I had no complaint. And it was plainly evident that neither had she. I think she would have liked to show me how she made the thing work. It was none of my business—customers were waiting—but I have often wished that I had asked her. There was the matter of space. The tenement could not possibly have contained more than five rooms—more likely there were only four. The attic was a half-story affair, lacking side windows—there may have been a little space up there. And there was the matter of money. Seventeen people, and only two of them wage earners. Twenty-five dollars a week for the pair at the most optimistic outside.

Of course, a few years later, when a dozen or so of the youngsters were in the mill, the old folks would touch affluence. Why, within ten years they could retire. But not permanently. The kids would marry and establish multitudinous dynasties of their own. No—the husband would stick to his loom until he was a gnarled old man, and then heaven knows what would happen to him. Or to her.

Well, it is allowable to dream. Perhaps the older children's sacrifices may have enabled one or two of the younger to get a good education. Perhaps one of them is today a prosperous doctor, another a more prosperous lawyer, and the old folks have been rewarded with a little white cottage out Scituate way, with morning-glories climbing up the back porch. Perhaps.

Altogether I enumerated something better than two thousand men, women, and children, and probably two or three dollars' worth of horses. I got a government check for more than fifty dollars. It was the largest sum of money I had ever received in one lump.

XII

Door to Door Once More

,

SOME aluminum people—*the* aluminum people, undoubtedly—used to send a representative to Brown University every spring to recruit likely students to serve as salesmen during the summer vacation. The selected students were not to go around punching doorbells and inquiring: "Madam, could I interest you in a new type of double boiler?" Nothing so crude, so direct, as that. The aluminum company representative told his candidates that the thing to do was to hire a meeting place of some sort and announce in the local press that a lecture on dietetics (a sort of new word then) was to be given in such-and-such a hall on such-and-such a date by so-and-so. Usually some women's organization was signed up to sponsor the meeting. The student-speaker was to start out with a few elementary facts about digestion and dietetics, edging in the latter with a sort of of-course-we-all-know-what-dietetics-is suggestion, and then he would gradually work around to the subject of aluminumware. Of course, he would say, he had nothing against kitchen utensils made of something else, only he had, it turned out, quite a bit. He was to wind up by giving simple demonstrations and saying he would be delighted to answer any questions regarding dietetics and incidentally was prepared to give special private demonstrations of these marvelous new cooking devices at the homes of members of the club, or even at the homes of a few carefully selected nonmembers. Within a few days he would have become a straight-out aluminum salesman, but very few people would have noticed the change, so he would still be socially acceptable and, if he were particularly clever, would thereafter be remembered in the community, by some of the people at least, as the pleasant young college man who gave that interesting talk on dietetics.

This sort of thing, I could see, was not up my alley at all. I did not like the idea of standing up before an audience of women and trying to tell them how to cook. My only reason for toying even momentarily with the aluminum idea was that if I became a champion of dietetics I could choose, within reason, any territory I wanted. Up to that time I had never been farther west or south than Hoboken or farther east or north than Boston. I particularly wanted to go up the Hudson to Cold Spring, a village fifty-four miles north of New York to which my Aunt Bertha and Uncle Gilbert had moved a few years before. Aunt Bertha had sent us exciting accounts of the beauties of the Highlands of the Hudson—Cro'nest and Mount Taurus (or, if you choose, as I do, Bull Hill) and Breakneck Mountain and Storm King. Moreover, she and Uncle Gib had no children and always liked having a niece or a nephew visit them. I thought it would be quite pleasant to take over the Cold Spring territory and sell something, anything, with Aunt Bertha's house as a base. If I proved a failure as a salesman (and I suspected the worst) I would at least be sure of bed and board and good company.

The man from the aluminum company was not the only scout who came to Brown looking for salesmen—he was simply the highest-powered. There were half a dozen others, but of these I recall only the man who was signing up students to sell *The Century Book of Facts*. This was a sort of one-volume encyclopedia published by a company in Springfield, Massachusetts. In its cheapest binding of stout buckram it sold for three dollars, half of which went to the salesman. The more elaborate bindings cost up to seven dollars and a half, as I remember, and the com-

The delightful creatures appeared out of nowhere like a particularly agitated cumulus cloud.

mission was higher, both absolutely and proportionately. Salesmen for *The Century Book of Facts* would not be required to lecture or to give demonstrations; they were simply to go from house to house extolling the merits of the work, and stressing its educational value if there were children in the family. The only piece of equipment the salesman had to carry was a prospectus which displayed samples of the different kinds of binding and contained, at the back, several ruled blank pages on which intending purchasers were to inscribe their names. The prospectus could be concealed under the coat without too much awkwardness, but even carried in the hand it was not likely to alarm the prospect unduly, since it merely made the salesman look like someone from the water department.

Accordingly I cast my lot with *The Century Book of Facts* man on his promise to allot me the Cold Spring area exclusively. I prepared to leave home a few days after the end of the college year. When the day of departure—a Saturday—arrived I packed a straw suitcase and took the Joy Line steamer to New York. This was to be my longest trip away from home in all my life thus far, both in distance traveled and time elapsed, for I planned to stay most of the summer. Every householder in Cold Spring could not be supplied with *The Century Book of Facts* in a day.

Financially I had cut things rather fine. I had enough money with me to get a good substantial twenty-five-cent breakfast in New York and to pay my fare (fifty cents) from New York to Cold Spring on the Hudson River Day Line. The Joy Line docked only a few piers distant from the Day Line. I reached New York in good season, seven-thirty or so, had a hearty meal somewhere down on West Street, and then went over to inspect the financial district, lugging the straw suitcase with me. At that time of day, on that first day of the week, in that season of the year, and in that year of recorded history, Wall Street presented a picture of almost sanctified calm.

I was under the impression, how arrived at I cannot now recall, that the Cold Spring boat left at ten o'clock. By nine-thirty I was at the pier. It seemed oddly deserted for a bright summer Sunday morning. The Cold Spring boat, I was informed, had sailed at nine o'clock.

I knew I did not have enough money to get to Cold Spring by train. The train trip, at two cents a mile, would have come to a bit over a dollar. I did not have a dollar. There was probably some way—elevated or subway or surface car—whereby I could work my way a considerable distance north (since New York's transportation system was famous for giving fantastically long rides for a nickel) and then, if all worked well, have enough money to complete the trip by rail. There would, of course, be no more eating until I reached Cold Spring.

I put my problem before a chance pedestrian on West Street. Unlike most persons thus accosted, whether in New York, Shanghai, Bordeaux, or Grant's Corners, this gentleman gave explicit, complete, and readily comprehensible directions which worked out to the letter.

Adopting his program, I walked east with my suitcase and took a Third Avenue elevated train. At the end of the line (and I am a little vague as to exactly where that may have been in the summer of 1910) I went down to the street and set out afoot for Woodlawn. At my left, for a mile or two or five hundred, I had the high stone escarpment that bounds Woodlawn Cemetery. Today I never look upon that beetling redoubt from a New Haven train without wiping from my forehead a recollected bead of perspiration.

I reached Woodlawn weary and winded and armsore. Few edifices in the world (I have yet to see the Taj Mahal) have ever looked so beautiful to me as did Woodlawn railroad station that Sunday noon. It had seats and a roof, and open windows through which a delicious breeze was sweeping. After a short rest I went

out to the terminal of the Yonkers line and took a trolley to
Getty Square, obtaining a transfer (as instructed) to Hastings.
Thus I got from lower Manhattan to Hastings, a distance of
twenty miles, for ten cents. I walked down the hill to Hastings
station (not nearly so fine a building as Woodlawn station) and
inspected the timetable posted near the ticket window. The next
train scheduled to stop at Cold Spring was due in three quarters
of an hour.

I let more than two of those three quarters go by before I could
summon the courage to ask the ticket agent what the fare to
Cold Spring was. I knew I should have to ask in just that way.
I would not dare say, "One to Cold Spring," because if I did not
have enough money to pay for it, it would be terribly embarrassing. I could, of course, have patted my pockets and said, "Dear
me, blest if I haven't lost my wallet!" but I have never been good
at that sort of thing. On the other hand, by asking, "What is the
fare to Cold Spring?", in the event that the trip was beyond my
means I could say, "Thank you—I just wanted to know—I may
run up there some day to visit an aunt." This would have
sounded a little silly, but I suspect ticket agents have to listen to
sillier things every day, even at Hastings station.

When I finally put it to the touch my difficulties immediately
vanished. By postponing the inquiry I had simply given myself a
needless half-hour of misery. I had enough for the ride and eight
cents over.

At Cold Spring I had to ask the way to Aunt Bertha's house,
because she would be expecting me by boat, and the boat was not
due for an hour or more. The house was not far from the station,
between the railroad and the river—the back yard, indeed, slid
down into the river. (The house is still there, only today it is the
office of an oil company whose tankers discharge near by.)
From the back door there was a breath-taking prospect of the
Highlands, with Cro'nest rearing its massive bastion skyward,

across the water, and beyond it the softer contours of Storm King. Downstream, tree-covered Constitution Island stuck out just far enough to hide the buildings of the United States Military Academy at West Point. I could have spent fascinated hours watching river traffic swing around the end of the island and head for the broad expanse of Newburgh Bay. I could have and I did, to the detriment of my career as a book salesman. But how compare explaining to a Cold Spring housewife the merits of *The Century Book of Facts* to the thrill of seeing the *Mary Powell,* the loveliest river craft ever fashioned, cleave the dark waters in the shadow of Cro'nest with her gleaming white prow?

Aunt Bertha and Uncle Gib were delighted to see me even if I was a little ahead of schedule. I gave them an account of my adventures and presently sat down to a supper of cold sliced pot roast, potato salad, homemade chili-sauce, homemade biscuits, butter, homemade doughnuts, and coffee laced with condensed milk. That is one meal the details of which are not likely ever to elude my memory.

Since these memorabilia are concerned with my economic history during the first twenty-one years of my life I must, in all honesty, set down the blunt details of my stewardship as salesman of *The Century Book of Facts.* I spent nearly the whole summer in Cold Spring and I sold two books, both in the buckram binding. My first sale was to a widow who took in washing and had two daughters in school. My last was to a retired Army colonel who lived on a magnificent estate and owned at least a dozen pointers. I walked up the long driveway and onto the broad front porch of the mansion and was immediately surrounded by these delightful creatures, who appeared out of nowhere like a particularly agitated cumulus cloud. They were the soul of amiability. They slapped their whip-lash tails against my legs and licked my hands and the prospectus indiscriminately.

The colonel came to the door, issued a peremptory command to the pointers which produced absolutely no result, and asked me what I wanted. I opened up on my sales talk and started to display my prospectus. The pointers would have none of this business. Neither would the colonel. He halted me brusquely.

"Leave that with me and call for it in the morning."

This, of course, was about the same thing as asking a plumber to leave his wrench. Still, it would give me an excuse to knock off for the day, so I handed him the prospectus. I duly called at the mansion the following morning. There was no sign of the colonel or of the pointers—they were probably out pointing, and *en echelon,* too, if the colonel had anything to say about it. A neatly uniformed maid answered my ring and gave me back my prospectus. So the old warhorse didn't have the nerve to turn me down in person! A little later, stumbling futilely through another sales talk and flipping over the pages of the prospectus in the process, I happened to reach the almost virgin first sheet on the section of blank pages reserved for orders. The washwoman's name no longer stood alone.

The literate colonel was not my only point of contact with the military establishment that summer. One afternoon I visited West Point, making the journey on a small launch whose owner operated it as a ferry. He who has not seen Retreat at West Point has missed one of the most soul-stirring spectacles that this land has to offer. I saw Retreat, that first time, under particularly favorable circumstances. West Point was comparatively inaccessible in those days. There were no busloads of tourists up from New York, no cars bearing the license tags of the forty-eight states. I am glad that today the citizenry can take in Retreat in such quantities, but I am equally glad that I enjoyed my own initiation to the ceremony in an approximate privacy. Of the handful of spectators who were present I recall only a presumable Civil War veteran who, as the flag slid down the staff, placed his hat to his bosom and gazed unflinchingly into the sunset. A tingle shot up and down my spinal cord and I felt fully three thousand percent American. God was in his heaven and all was well with the Union, even if the plump and amiable occupant of the White House did happen to be a Republican.

In the files of gray-and-white-clad cadets who strode stiffly and splendidly by, there were some whom destiny had marked for her own (if destiny actually does any marking, and a good many soldiers, particularly those who get to hear guns go off, find some degree of comfort in maintaining that she does). There were certain others present who, for my money (and for yours too, O fellow-taxpayer), would remain little better than public charges for the rest of their military careers. But strike the balance, assess the average, and it is vastly to the good. Let us lift the veil of the future (which is no trouble at all, without benefit of destiny, after this interval) and see who some of these youngsters are and what they are going to do.

Here is Cadet Bradford G. Chynoweth. Thirty-two years from now, a brigadier general, he will be a prisoner of war of the Japanese, taken in the fall of the Philippines, and he will remain in enemy hands for more than three years.

Here is Cadet William H. Wilbur who, just before his promotion from colonel to brigadier general thirty-two years later, will receive his country's highest award for valor, the Congressional Medal of Honor, for a series of exploits in the North African landing. Read his citation: "On November 8, 1942, he landed at Fedala with the leading assault waves where opposition had developed into a firm and continuous defensive line across his route of advance. Commandeering a vehicle, he was driven toward the hostile defenses under incessant fire, finally locating a French officer who accorded him passage through the forward positions. He then proceeded in total darkness through sixteen miles of enemy occupied country intermittently subjected to heavy bursts of fire and accomplished his mission by delivering his letters to appropriate French officials in Casablanca. Returning toward his command, Colonel Wilbur detected a hostile battery firing effectively on our troops. He took charge of a platoon of American tanks and personally led them in an attack and capture of the battery."

Here is Cadet Millard F. Harmon, who in 1917 will become one of America's first combat pilots. Twenty-five years later, after commanding Army Air and Ground Forces in the campaign for the Solomons, he will be named Commanding General of United States Army Forces in the South Pacific Area. In March, 1945, he will make his final flight into the unknown, and a year later will be officially declared dead.

Here is Cadet Brehon Burke Somervell, who in 1918 will win the Distinguished Service Cross for an exploit during the Meuse-Argonne campaign, the greatest battle ever fought up to that time by American troops: "Voluntarily serving on the staff of the Eighty-ninth Division, he conducted the first engineering reconnaissance of the damaged bridges at Pouilly, where with two scouts he advanced more than two hundred meters beyond the American outposts, crossing three branches of the Meuse River and successfully encountering the enemy." In the Second World War, with the rank of general, he will command the world-wide operations of the Army Service Forces.

Here is Cadet Carl Spatz. He, too, will become one of his country's first military pilots, and will receive the Distinguished Service Cross for bravery in France in 1918: "Although he had received orders to go to the United States, he begged for and received permission to serve with a pursuit squadron at the front. Knowing that another attack was to take place in the vicinity of

Verdun, he remained on duty in order to take part. On the day of the attack west of the Meuse, while with his patrol over enemy lines, a number of enemy aircraft were encountered. In the combat that followed he succeeded in bringing down two enemy planes. In his ardor and enthusiasm he became separated from his patrol while following another enemy far beyond the lines. His gasoline giving out, he was forced to land, and managed to land within friendly territory." Nine years later, in the era of boom and bust, he will be awarded the Distinguished Flying Cross for keeping the airplane "Question Mark" in the air over southern California for one hundred and fifty hours, fifty minutes, and fifteen seconds—seventeen hours, nine minutes, and forty-five seconds short of a full week. In 1937, weary of hearing himself called "Spats," he will add a second *a* to his name and be called "Spots." In 1943 he will assume command of United States Army Air Forces in the North African Theatre, and, in 1944, of the United States Strategic Air Forces in the European Theatre. Two years later he will be appointed Commanding General, Army Air Forces.

Here is Cadet Alexander McCarrell Patch, who as an infantry officer will participate in three major operations in France in 1918. In 1942 he will command Army, Navy, and Marine units on Guadalcanal in the Solomons. In 1944 he will assume command of the Seventh American Army in Sicily, and will remain with it throughout the operations in France and Germany that are to follow. He will return to the United States to die of pneumonia at Fort Sam Houston in March, 1945. Thirty-two years after this Retreat ceremony of 1910 another Alexander McCarrell Patch will receive his commission as second lieutenant under the Victory Monument at the northern end of the parade ground and will move at once into the final testing school of battle. On October 20, 1944, he will be killed in action in Alsace while serving as an infantry captain with his father's Seventh Army.

That first visit to West Point was made, as I say, in 1910. I should have gone back the following year and watched the workout of a couple of plebes named Omar N. Bradley and Dwight D. Eisenhower.

XIII

Clio and Aunt Bertha

I T IS not my intention to clutter up these recollections with relations, poor or otherwise, interesting or uninteresting, characters or straight men, but I should like to ask the reader's indulgence while I introduce him to Aunt Bertha. For Aunt Bertha, it seems to me, merits inclusion here for a special reason which will, I hope, emerge in the process of presenting her.

I never heard Aunt Bertha mention Clio, that one among the Muses who, "singing of famous deeds," in the words of Ausonius, "restores the past to life." Aunt Bertha was born in La Grange, Georgia, on March 20, 1857. Her father was a Rhenish Prussian fresco painter who had left home following the yeast and seethe of '48 and had found in America not only freedom of soul and speech but also a gentle and comely Württemberg girl whom he soon married. This worthy couple became my paternal grandparents, a fact of no interest to Clio but of considerable moment to Aunt Bertha, my father, and me.

The gentle and comely Württemberger lived into my time—a plump little creature with dark gray hair parted squarely in the middle and combed severely down at the sides. If she ever sat otherwise than with her hands folded austerely in her lap (taken with the even part in her hair, this posture gave her the conventionalized symmetry of an Egyptian figurine), I do not remember it. After fifty years of life in the States, Confederate and United, she still had a strong German accent, but one rarely heard it, because she spoke little. She had left her husband in a Southern grave two years after Appomattox. He was in his thirty-ninth year.

My father, in that distant time, was little more than two years old. Aunt Bertha was almost ten. She represented, therefore, the only vocal link existing between my grandfather and me. Aunt Bertha took after her father, I am sure, in more ways than one. She was five feet nine and straight as a guardsman. She was forthright, downright, and upright. So, I am certain, was he.

I was much older than I should have been (it was, in fact, long after my summer of bookselling in Cold Spring) before it occurred to me that Aunt Bertha was what the historians, the godsons of Clio, denominate a primary source. It had been interesting to listen to her fragmentary and casual recollections of a grandparent who had left the world twenty-four years before I entered it—to speculate therefrom if I might have drawn anything from his character across the interval of a generation, something for the transfer of which my father stood, as it were, in the office of trustee. Aunt Bertha could be of little help here— neither could Solomon have been. And then, as I say, it occurred to me that Aunt Bertha was something more than a mere aunt—she was an alert, observing, ratiocinating entity whose childhood had lain in a momentous epoch and in a spot of earth charged with emotion and conflict.

I do not altogether do myself justice when I intimate that this flagrantly obvious conclusion came to me with the blast of inspiration. One of Aunt Bertha's earliest recollections (and the very first I can recall her imparting to me) had been so palpably adulterate that I decided that anything out of her memoirs must be suspect. At the age of four or so, she insisted, she had been chased by a hoopsnake. It was the fashion of the hoopsnake to stick his tail into his mouth, convert himself into a sort of bicycle

"This is my father's property!" she cried.

tire, roll straight and true at his victim and transfix him with his
suddenly released tail. One could best hope to meet this awful
menace by backing against a tree and skittling out of the way,
matador fashion, when the creature struck. His tail thereby became embedded in the tree beyond likelihood of extraction. One
was then privileged to dispatch him at leisure.

Now the hoopsnake, in sober herpetology, simply does not
exist. Mermaids and unicorns and griffons there may be. There
are no hoopsnakes. Useless to attempt to convince Aunt Bertha
of this. Of course there were hoopsnakes. She had been chased by
a hoopsnake. All that this signified, of course, was that when
Aunt Bertha was on the threshold out of infancy she had heard
the prowess and qualifications of the hoopsnake recited with
such convincing gusto (possibly by someone who had become
convinced in the same fashion) that the fable affixed itself to her
consciousness as her own experience.

Aunt Bertha's loyal adherence to the hoopsnake myth long
vitiated my faith in the validity of her memory—of her capacity
to sing, like Clio, of famous deeds and to restore the past to life.
(I had forgotten that Herodotus, the very father of history, told
much worse whoppers, and heaven knows *he* had Clio's bless-
ing.) Two subsequent incidents, however, revitalized my faith.

First was the case of Uncle Steve. Uncle Steve was my grandfather's slave. Aunt Bertha (in my childhood she was brown-
haired, brown-eyed and handsome; at eighty-five she was still
brown-eyed and handsome) never mentioned Uncle Steve until
I was pretty well grown up. That was my fault. A native of
Connecticut, and reared while the Grand Army of the Republic
was slipping noiselessly away from perihelion, I never appreciated (and would not have dared appreciate openly if I had
thought of it) my authentic if somewhat remote Southern background. I had voted for a President of the United States (a native
Virginian, and he was twice elected) before I set foot on soil

more austral than New York's Battery Park. But as the Civil, or Between the States, War slid into historical perspective, the Lost Cause (which has won in all the novels) took on a roseate patina, and it became ineffably respectable, even well north of the Battery, to have Southern blood, Southern connections, a Southern accent. And to be able to say that one's forebears had owned slaves—

So I asked Aunt Bertha if her father had owned slaves.

"We had one," she said. "Uncle Steve. He ate just as well as the rest of us."

"Are you sure you had just the one?"

"Only Uncle Steve."

This was patently the truth, but, like so much truth, it was also gall and wormwood. One cannot go about proclaiming that one's grandfather owned *a* slave. Does one boast of an unique glove, a solitary earring, a widowed andiron, an odd volume of Gibbon? I tried vainly to detach Aunt Bertha from this ridiculous and equivocal position.

"Sometimes a slave was parcelled out among several families, wasn't he, just as farmers combine to buy a tractor, or commuters a power lawn mower? Didn't grandfather own even a fractional interest in some slave beside Uncle Steve?"

My reasoning here, I admit, was highly disingenuous. Mathematically, one and one-sixth slaves would be plural, so that I could say, if anyone asked me (and I should have seen to it that someone did ask me), "Oh, yes, we owned slaves."

"No," Aunt Bertha replied, "we only had Uncle Steve."

This was a devastating disappointment. But the incident established Aunt Bertha as a competent witness, and more than atoned for the hoopsnake.

The episode of the Confederate general strengthened Aunt Bertha's credibility immeasurably—nay, so far as I was concerned, perfected it. I had asked her idly if she had ever seen any soldiers in the neighborhood. The family had moved from Georgia to Marion, Alabama, just before the outbreak of war.

"General Walthall and Captain Kouraysh used to visit father sometimes, and they would talk over things we children weren't allowed to hear."

This sounded amusing—my single-slave-owning, fresco-painting grandsire entertaining a Confederate brass hat and discussing the higher strategy with him in indeterminate English. Obviously the general was just another hoopsnake. But some impulse sent me to the *Dictionary of American Biography,* and there, in Volume XIX, was a whole page about Edward Cary Walthall, set forth by Professor Charles S. Sydnor of Duke University (like Aunt Bertha, a native Georgian). Walthall, born in Richmond, Virginia, grew up in Mississippi, became by due process of training a lawyer, joined the Yalobusha Rifles when his great war came (how I wish my grandfather might have been affiliated with the Yalobusha Rifles!), and was promoted brigadier in 1863. Professor Sydnor says Walthall was "several times matched against General George H. Thomas," which must have been a whole military career in itself. One could readily accept the statement that he "became noted for his dependability and resourcefulness when outnumbered or when his army was being forced to retreat." Wounded at Missionary Ridge, he remained in the saddle; in the Tennessee campaign soon afterward two horses were shot from under him. A year before the war ended he won a deserved promotion to major general. Early in the ensuing turmoil of peace he met Lucius Quintus Cincinnatus Lamar; a warm friendship developed, and the two were largely instrumental in restoring order in Mississippi. When Lamar, then United States Senator, became President Cleveland's Secretary of the Interior in March, 1885, Walthall was appointed to succeed him, and save for a brief hiatus due to ill health he continued in the Senate until his death in 1898 at the age of sixty-seven.

My respect for Aunt Bertha as a primary source was now immovably fixed. She had no idea what the meetings with General Walthall and Captain Kouraysh were about, and would not bolster my attempts to impart to the colloquies a glamorous atmosphere—something to do with espionage, or at least some mysterious sort of intelligence work.

Captain Kouraysh would have fitted into this picture cozily enough. I spell the name as Aunt Bertha pronounces it; the accent is strongly on the last syllable. (She seems never to have seen it in print or writing.) Could it actually have been Captain Courage, uttered with some slight concession to Gallicization? And could "Captain Courage" have been the glittering incognito of some dashing beau sabreur who hid his flambeau under a bushel, some unsung Dixie D'Artagnan?

I am afraid not. In civil life Captain Kouraysh, however he may have spelled himself, operated a distillery. Aunt Bertha was sure of that. It is a calling that does not necessarily unfit one for high emprises, but Captain Kouraysh's distillery was right in Marion (or perhaps Selma), and he himself apparently lived in the neighborhood all his life, or at least during all of the life that Aunt Bertha lived there. Her most romantic recollection of him (and the majority of men have slenderer claims to the attribute) was that he could make a whacking rum omelet, whereof my grandfather, a teetotaler, would not partake. Grandfather seems to have allowed the children to sample it, or perhaps Captain Kouraysh sneaked a bit to Aunt Bertha. He would have.

Whether these conferences with the commissioned personnel had anything to do with certain stealthy excavating activities on my grandfather's plantation I do not know, nor did Aunt

Bertha. One night she heard the clink of shovels on a hill near the house; investigating, she discovered a cluster of soldiers busily scooping out the earth.

"This is my father's property!" she cried. What an awareness of ownership children have!

A posted sentry, annoyed at having a march stolen on him by a snip in pigtails, brandished a firearm and sent her pelting back into the house. Somehow—she could not explain—she associated this incident with printing. She was too honest to essay any adventitious link. Were the soldiers constructing a cache for state papers, for currency, for bonds? Were they preparing to tuck a printing press away in a cave? Or was the association of printing in Aunt Bertha's mind idle and fortuitous, and was some cautious back-area commander of troops simply playing with a reserve trench system?

"I don't know," was Aunt Bertha's answer. "I was just a little girl. Father told me to keep away, and not to ask questions."

Much of her authenticity, indeed, inhered in her refusal to improvise. If she could not answer a question she would say regretfully: "Not that I know of," or "I can't recall whether he did or not," or "That I don't remember," or "I don't think so, but I might be wrong," or "I don't know—you see I was so young."

Her father was three times called to service, three times invalided home. The spirit was eager, the flesh pitifully weak. On one return he bore in triumph a can of coffee. I have an idea, independent of Aunt Bertha's recollection, that this event occurred on October 18, 1864, for that was the day on which my father was born, and he often told me (quoting his mother's testimony) that the first thing he ever drank was coffee. My belief is that while the bacchanalia was at its height a woman neighbor who had played midwife, or perhaps Captain Kouraysh (ah, it must have been Captain Kouraysh!), cried: "Let's give the little fellow a drop—he may never taste it again!"

Whence the coffee? Aunt Bertha hadn't the slightest idea. Foraged? Borrowed, in a manner of speaking, from an officers' mess? Captured from the well-provisioned Yankees? Nor could she recall whether the precious contents of the can was carefully rationed, or consumed in one wild orgy—a single grand *Kaffee-klatsch,* Southern style.

Anyway, the can was eventually emptied, whether in an hour, or days, or months. But keep your eye on it. It still has a part to play in the family drama.

The coffee shortage was the only enforced war economy which Aunt Bertha remembered. Perhaps, as a child of from four to eight, she should not have remembered even that. I suspect that she recalled rather the complaints of her elders. German born and reared, they must have missed their tipple as Uncle Steve would have missed his watermelon (of which there was an abundance). There were beef, pork, vegetables in plenty. There was little wheat, but Alabama ate and drank corn; there was little sugar, but this was a molasses era and a molasses country. Nor did folks want for clothing; Aunt Bertha thought she went barefoot much of the time, but she recalled vividly a pair of red shoes bought in Selma.

There must have been some lack of dietary balance, however; a baby brother and a baby sister, John and Maria, died sometime before 1864; my father became a second John. And Aunt Bertha attended the funeral of an infant whose pathetic little corpse became famous in local legendry as "the transparent baby." "You could see right through the body," declared Aunt Bertha, who must have had to stand tiptoe to inspect this tiny victim of malnutrition.

Propaganda in the schools? Excoriation of the Yankee? Brave words for Victoria, Napoleon III, General Lee?

"I don't think so," said Aunt Bertha. "There was a teacher who brought some honey for her dinner, and the bees found it, and we had to stay out of the room until they drove the bees away."

It was during one of her father's assignments with troops that a man came to find out how much cotton the family had. He had a mustache (a rarity in that full-bearded era) and wore a blue coat and white trousers. Did these constitute some sort of uniform? Aunt Bertha wasn't sure. There were two bales of cotton in the family storehouse, but Aunt Bertha's mother apparently did not report them. Recalling the shy little lady of thirty-five years later, I cannot imagine her actually denying that she had them. But as soon as the visitor had gone she reported the incident to the town marshal or the local military authority, and eight men were assigned to watch the house. Despite this precaution, or perhaps in collaboration with it, one bale vanished during the night. Next day Aunt Bertha herself had no trouble in tracing the bale, by means of the tufts torn off by brambles, to the heart of a thicket. Uncle Steve and casual helpers fetched it home, and that appears to have ended the incident. Was the mustachioed bluecoat a duly appointed representative of the civil or military authorities, empowered to commandeer the crop? Was the subsequent theft executed at his orders, with the connivance of the local authorities? Aunt Bertha did not know. But the episode seemed to reflect her only experience of the lawlessness that accompanies war, or perhaps of the lawlessness that war itself inevitably legalizes.

There was an end of war at last, and the men who had fought for the bonnie blue flag (Aunt Bertha used the phrase without affectation) came home. Aunt Bertha, along with other children, stood on the seminary steps to see them march by, and little Frances Sellick climbed to the flat top of one of the stone posts for a better view. It was a tatterdemalion company that passed, plodding along at ragged route step—one-armed men, one-legged men, men with matted hair on their heads and matted clothes on their backs, listless men, dazed men, battered human driftwood washed up beyond reach of the ebbing tides of disaster. Suddenly a ragged, bearded fellow broke ranks and rushed toward the stone post on which Frances Sellick was sitting. He reached up, grasped her in his arms, ran back into formation with her. Her screams echoed back down the road as the line wound on—echoed back, Aunt Bertha is sure, even after the bedraggled veteran had been able to convince Frances that he was her father.

Grandfather was not in this group. His third and final return from the front must have occurred sometime earlier. Toward the end he drove into Selma with his cotton.

"There was a lot of it," says Aunt Bertha. "It was worth either six hundred or six thousand dollars."

He left it with a broker named, she thought, Gold. "Father trusted him." Some days later he sought out Gold to learn if he had marketed the cotton. Two strangers were in charge of the warehouse. "They told father Mr. Gold had gone to New Orleans and wouldn't come back. They said, "We don't know anything about your cotton.'"

And that was that. No worse for grandfather, perhaps, than for others. Uncle Steve hung on—where else could he go?

"Five days before the war ended" (I am uncertain exactly what Aunt Bertha meant by the phrase) her father sold his plantation to a Mrs. Day who was previously unreported in Aunt Bertha's recollections.

Grandfather sold the plantation not as a gesture of despair but because the condition of his lungs made it imperative for him to go north. That is what his doctor told him. The doctor was a vague and nameless entity to Aunt Bertha. Grandfather had consumption, and in those days one sought to cure consumption by running away from it, not realizing that instead one ran away with it.

The empty coffee can (carefully treasured for memory's sake) was brought out and stuffed with what Aunt Bertha, with a certain relish, called "the family jewels," plus a few carefully husbanded gold coins. Abandoning all else, the family set out— father, mother, daughters of nine and eight (the daughter of nine was Aunt Dora), a son of two (my father). Uncle Steve fell on his knees as they left and pleaded tearfully to be taken away. But there was not enough in the coffee can to share with Uncle Steve. My father passed on to me the recollection of his mother that the party stopped in Washington, where the three children were patted amiably on the head by President Andrew Johnson.

Their destination was Hoboken, where grandfather had an older sister—her son, fighting for the Union, had fallen in the Wilderness. ("A bullet hit him right between the eyes.") The Hoboken air, small wonder, did not improve grandfather's condition. A Yankee doctor, true to the medical conventions of his day, ordered the patient south.

"So we went back. Father died at Athens, Georgia, on February 9, 1867. They buried him on a hilltop."

His widow felt no urge to stay in the South. They all went back to Hoboken. Aunt Bertha carried away a final mélange of memories:

A blind white horse named Selim. (The last horse my father ever owned, who died in harness in 1916, was also blind and white and named Selim.)

A Mrs. Stonework, who dressed always in white and kept peacocks.

A Mr. Ryle. A Mrs. Couch. These survive in name only, detached from personality.

Uncle Albert and his wife—"Uncle Albert's wife was a Southern woman. She didn't speak German. One time she got so mad when father and Uncle Albert talked German that she had a slave take her two miles into the woods in a wheelbarrow. Uncle Albert had to go out there and apologize"—in English, one assumes. And did he have to trundle her back?

"What was it like, settling in the North after the war?" I asked Aunt Bertha.

"I felt funny, coming to a strange place."

And she told me how she sat on the front stoop of her aunt's Hoboken house, humming to herself. The hum broke into words:

> Jeff Davis is a gentleman, and Lincoln is a fool,
> Jeff Davis rides a milk-white horse, and Lincoln rides a mule.

A man came along the street and stopped to listen quizzically. He must have been a kindly soul, and certainly he was not waving a bloody shirt. Perhaps he knew that a boy had gone out of that house to die.

"You'd better not sing that around here, young lady, or somebody's liable to cut your head off."

Aunt Bertha ran into the house. It seems to have been her favorite method of eluding a dilemma.

"But I don't think now that Lincoln was a fool," she added. "I was only a little girl then."

XIV

Ring on My Finger

WEEK or so before Christmas of my junior year at Brown University somebody told me that Providence Post Office was hiring additional special delivery messengers for the holiday rush. I went to the post office, applied, was hired, and was told to report at six o'clock on the evening of December twenty-second. Payment would be eight cents for every letter or parcel taken out, whether delivered or not.

On the morning of the twenty-second I didn't feel so good. My throat was sore, and I winced when I touched myself. That afternoon, feverish and shivering, I lay down on a cot in the dormitory room of a classmate and managed to sleep a little—something I would normally never have dreamed of doing in the daytime. When I awakened I felt worse. My throat was even more gulpingly tender; swallowing hurt so much that I started swallowing harder than I ever had in my life.

At six o'clock I reported at the post office. This marked the only time to date that I have ever been behind a post office grill, but I was in no condition to appreciate this inside view of the mechanism of government. The building was almost brand new, and a mercury-vapor lighting system had been installed in its construction. As a result, all of the clerks wore a sickly green pallor which sorted ill with the zest and zip of their movements but which suited me perfectly.

Somebody gave me a handful of special delivery letters (I do not recall any packages) and I stumbled out in the direction of

South Providence. I remember that one of the letters was con-signed to somebody in the great Gothic bulk of Rhode Island Hospital, and I stood in the waiting room in an agony of misery while someone signed for the letter. If the hospital authorities had realized what a concentrated package of pestilence I repre-sented at the moment there would probably have been consider-able of a to-do.

I had about a dozen letters to deliver and the one for the hospital was perhaps the sixth, but I could do no more. The mails must go through, but not through me. I groped back to the post office, and once more felt right at home with the animated corpses who were bustling greenly about. I reported to my chief, whoever he was, and told him I couldn't go on. Some hint of my condition must have reached him through the sickly illumination, because he took my undelivered letters and told me to get along home.

I got along home—by trolley car, I suppose—and told my father and stepmother I felt terrible and was going to bed. I must have looked as bad as I felt, for I had barely got into bed, chattering teeth and all, when the family doctor appeared. His name was Burdick; he was benign and bald, and his round face hung over me like an amiable moon. A look down my throat, a glance at my fingertips, some general prodding and tapping, and he said I had diphtheria and scarlet fever.

A hospital for contagious diseases had opened in Providence only a few weeks before, and thither I was sent, for the good both of myself and of the general population. An ambulance was called and I was hauled out to it on a stretcher—to date my first such journey—and deposited on the floor. Above my misery, as we started off, I got a little thrill out of my first ambulance ride, and I tried (successfully, I believe) to guess where we were by the sound of the vehicle as it went over streets which I knew by heart down to the very pavement. It was no trouble following our course down Plainfield Street to Olneyville Square and across the square to the left turn into Valley Street. Thereafter I was in less familiar territory.

I was carried into the hospital and put to bed. A pleasant-faced nurse (it emerged later, that, like my stepmother, she was a native of Canada) came over to the bed carrying in one hand a gleaming metallic cylinder the size and shape of a small bicycle pump. She told me to turn my back to her, pulled down the coverings, and pulled up my nightshirt—I was well enough to feel considerable embarrassment about this.

"Children sometimes squirm when we do this and break the needle," the nurse said. I took this to mean that as a person of nineteen I was supposed not to squirm. The needle jabbed into my left buttock, and several thousand units of antitoxin shot into me. I was then instructed to go to sleep, which was no trouble at all.

Next morning I awakened, practically cured, in a room with windows on three sides. On two sides the windows disclosed the outside world, and on the third a corridor that ended with my room and the room opposite. Across the corridor, behind a similarly revealing window, a young man of no more than three, obviously in an advanced stage of convalescence, was dancing up and down in his crib and clutching his crotch. He began waving gaily at me with his free hand as soon as he saw that I saw him. He had light curly hair and a gay chuckle—as the doors of both our rooms were open, the chuckle was merrily audible. So, an instant later, was his lusty bellow of "I want the bottle!" He seemed to me to be a little too old (or a little too young) for such a requirement, but his behest was quickly obeyed by a nurse who bustled up with a white enamelled utensil. I envied the frank forthrightness of the young; it was hours before I could summon sufficient courage to make a like request, and then in a whisper. I have no recollection of whether I ate anything that

A young man of no more than three was dancing up and down
in his crib.

day or not—I recall only a marvelous sense of well-being above the belt, virtually no sore throat, and an abject, miserable need for the bottle. Two or three days later I was completely cured of this sanitary shyness, and could ring for a urinal or a bedpan as readily as I do today for a dry Martini.

On Christmas morning my father, stepmother, and three-year-old sister stood outside my window and we enjoyed a lively conversation that consisted of handwavings, dumb show, smiles, grins, ear-wiggles, and rudimentary lip reading. It was very pleasant—all was right with the world and Santa Claus still lived.

By this time I was moderately familiar with the hospital routine. I was in the isolation ward, where each patient had a room to himself because he had two or more contagious diseases to himself. Most of the combinations were measles and chicken-pox. As a sufferer from both diphtheria and scarlet fever who was almost old enough to vote, I was easily the most notable patient in the ward in the eyes of the medical staff. As the senior male patient, or any other kind, by probably ten years, I was also the most important inmate in the eyes of the nurses. It is only fair to say that I did not attempt to take advantage of this situation. Neither did the nurses.

For instance, there was Miss B——. Miss B—— was a pupil nurse from Fall River and had the night trick. Every evening after she had taken over she would come in and sit down and talk to me—the rest of the ward was by this time sound asleep. One evening she looked across at the brightly lighted T.B. ward, in full view beyond my left-hand window, where another pupil nurse was looking out one of *her* windows.

"That's Fitzsimmons," said Miss B——. "If she was here she'd hold hands with you."

I was little skilled at the time in the technique of what has been mischristened the tender passion, but the utter lack of subtlety in this approach could hardly have been lost on my little play-mate Curlytop, across the corridor. Miss B—— attempted no follow-up, having obviously gone as far as a lady could go in the premises.

"That's a pretty ring you've got," I said after a few minutes of silence. I reached for her hand and held it for a moment. It was as responsive as a beanbag. Sometime after, but not too long, it occurred to Miss B—— that her hand was being held. She detached it from mine without rancor, and read me a quiet lecture. Then we talked for an hour, and the same every evening, except for the handholding, as long as Miss B—— was on night duty. That should have taught me all I needed to know about rings, or handholding. But it didn't.

During the day I was tended by graduate nurses (though by now I required little tending). One of these was nicknamed Speedy, by reason of her alertness, competence, and general capacity for accomplishing any given task in the least possible time. She was short, plump, good-natured, and unruffleable. She wore the blue-and-gold badge of Bellevue Hospital—I knew enough to be tremendously impressed by this.

Speedy and I got on splendidly together. It was Speedy who escorted Dr. Richardson, the superintendent, to my room when *he* escorted Dr. Chapin, health commissioner of Providence (for whom the hospital has since been renamed), on a tour of the recently opened institution. Dr. Chapin was himself a Brown man and we had a few minutes' talk about the college, and I was loud in my praise of the hospital. It was Speedy who brought me the package from Professor Albert Knight Potter—a package which contained Sir Walter Scott's *Quentin Durward*, Henry Harland's *The Cardinal's Snuff-Box*, Elihu Vedder's *The Digressions of V*, and a jar of calf's-foot jelly, all of which I consumed with high relish. It was Speedy, who, when I was adjudged able to get up, not only brought me a long pair of ladies' black stockings (something which a later age would call a gag, because I certainly had no need of them), but also watched me closely as I sat on the edge of the bed, put a tentative foot to the floor (how the needles did prick!), and steadied me as I woozily stood up for the first time in three weeks. Speedy steered me to an armchair and I plopped into it gratefully, while Saturn's rings whirled and clanged in my brainpan. Thirty seconds or so of that and everything cleared, and I looked at Speedy and thought she was the nicest of the several nice people I had met since I had set out for South Providence with a handful of special delivery letters—and what a hell of a long time ago *that* had been!

I stayed in the hospital two weeks longer, mainly for the good of society. My throat was examined daily. Three negative cultures were necessary for discharge. I had quite a succession of two-to-one decisions, and began to think I was destined to be the male diphtheria counterpart of Typhoid Mary. But at last I came through three for none.

For the first and last time I walked down the corridor between the neat little windowed rooms I knew were there but had never seen, save for my own and Curlytop's. Curlytop had departed with a cheery farewell chuckle days earlier, and had been replaced by a dark, silent, hollow-eyed, antisocial little girl who refused to respond to my waves. There had been two deaths in my final days in the ward, one in the room next to me. The ward was no longer the pleasant place where my raging throat had first become manageable overnight.

Speedy supervised the terminal paperwork and walked with me to a stairway which, it appeared, I had to go down under my own power. She put out her hand. I took it.

"Good-bye," she said. "Write to me and tell me how you're getting on."

I said I would, and started down the stairs. At the turn I

looked back. Speedy was still standing at the top. I waved clumsily, and she waved.

"Good-bye, Speedy," I said.

"Good-bye. Write soon."

I wrote. She wrote.

I had little difficulty getting back into the college routine. I had had the wit to fall ill at the very beginning of the Christmas vacation, and had simply enjoyed a somewhat more extended holiday than my less fortunate fellows.

A week or so after I had got back into the swing of things I went out to see Speedy. I waited for her at the hospital entrance—the end of the long lane which led down from the red-brick buildings. She came down it with her pert, alert little stride, white shoes and stockings gleaming in the dusk under the dark cape she had thrown over her uniform.

"Hello," she said.

I said, "Hello."

We walked up Eaton Street, then a country lane with open fields and a few moth-eaten estates bordering it. One of the estates was bounded by a long, low stone wall with a smooth flat top. On this we sat and talked about what I was doing and what she was doing and about the other nurses. The time passed pleasantly, and so it did on several subsequent occasions.

One evening when I was holding Speedy's hand, having acquired the knowledge of how not to do it from Miss B——, I began idly to twirl a ring she wore. This led the conversation around to rings, and Speedy took off her ring and put it on the ring finger of my left hand. There was no symbolism in this. I couldn't get the ring off. Speedy said not to worry—get the ring off at home where I'd have plenty of light and bring it back next time. So we talked about what I was doing and what she was doing and about the other nurses. I took Speedy back to the hospital entrance and said good night.

On the trolley car going home I began working on the ring. Outside of swelling the knuckle and abrading the base of the finger I accomplished nothing. I decided to let matters rest until next morning. At breakfast, which I usually ate quickly, and ate quicker than usual this time, I kept my left hand in my lap. I didn't want any of the folks to say, "Why, where did you get that ring?" I had done nothing to be ashamed of, nothing that was anybody's business but Speedy's and my own. I could, of course, have said that I had found it, but at that time I had a constitutional objection to lying, and I have never been able to do it well. I was particularly concerned lest my kid sister discover the ring and coo about it. I got out of the house as fast as I could.

That day I did not pay as much attention as I should have to Professor Walter Cochrane Bronson's exegesis of Milton's conception of the universe or to Professor William MacDonald's analysis of the Dred Scott decision. It was during Billy Mac's lecture that a temporary solution of my difficulty occurred to me. When I got home that night I made straight for the rag-bag and extracted a scrap of clean linen, which I bound neatly around the beringed finger.

At dinner my little sister said, "Oooooo, you cut your finger!"

If I had said yes, that would have been lying. I merely laughed and waved my left hand airily and asked her what she had been doing all day. This brought on a monologue which lasted all through the meal. My awareness of the operation of the feminine mind had increased vastly during the past few weeks.

But I couldn't go around with a permanent rag on my finger. I could file the ring off, or have somebody file it off for me (at some slight cuticular expense, certainly), but I did not intend to be a cad at my age—if a lady had lent me a ring it should be returned to her in good order, somehow.

My interesting condition had got noised about the Brown campus by this time, and several impractical and even ribald suggestions for remedying the situation were advanced. Rub the finger with lard. Butter. Sewing-machine oil. Soap. Sandpaper. Loop a wire through the ring (and then what?). Do nothing for a week, then start all over—you got it on, didn't you?

I cannot recall the name of the genius who finally released me from my predicament. I can, in fact, recall nothing about him except that he existed—perhaps I was too fascinated by his ingenuity and his dexterity to note any other attributes. He was, certainly, a fellow-student, because he delivered me from my bondage in the Brown Union one morning before chapel, and any intruder would have been recognized as such on sight. Nor have I any idea how he happened to know about me, except that everybody did know.

"Let's see that finger," he demanded rather than requested.

I stuck it out. He wiggled the ring.

"That's a cinch. Got a piece of string?"

I said no, but I'd get some. A student clerk in the college bookstore downstairs gave me a piece. I came back and handed the string to my benefactor.

Here is what he did (and if this is my only legacy to the world I think it will be sufficient as long as people put rings on their fingers and are unable to get them off): He pushed the ring down to the base of the finger. With the tip of a match he jammed one end of the string between the ring and the finger, and drew five or six inches of the string through. He then wound the rest of the string, closely and tightly, around the base of the finger and well up over the knuckle, much as if he were winding up a top. The tip of the finger was by now completely numb and strongly violet in color. But the genius was aware of that, and worked quickly. Bidding me hold the finger up straight, he took the loose end of string that he had inserted between ring and finger and pulled it gently toward him.

The ring began to move. As loop after loop of the string fell away, the ring rose up the finger, up and up, up and over the constricted knuckle, and, as I lowered my finger, the ring dropped off. So, almost, did the finger. I shook the finger, flexed it, wiggled it, rubbed it, licked it, and I thanked my Samaritan.

A few days later I got a check from the United States Government for, I think, a dollar and four cents.

A few years later Speedy married a doctor.

XV

Two Bells and Away We Go

THE day after I became a bachelor of arts (my so-called sheepskin had been handed to me by President William Herbert Perry Faunce of Brown University in the First Baptist Meeting House in Providence, "built for the Publick worship of Almighty God; and also for holding Commencements in"—built, too, from the proceeds of a Publick lottery)— the day after I became a bachelor of arts I went to the offices of the Rhode Island Company and was hired as a trolley-car conductor at the beginner's rate of twenty-one and three-quarters cents an hour. I was going back to college in September, but I had run up a few small debts and I wanted to pay these off and have a little left over.

I was sent to the Olneyville carhouse, given a book of rules, a fare-collector, a pad of transfers, a transfer-punch, and a number plate for my hat. The number was 642. A uniform was not compulsory for three months (in order to give a newcomer time to save up for it, I suppose). Since I was not going to be around that long, all I had to have was the hat—as with the gas company, the hat *was* the uniform. By a stroke of luck I was able to buy a hat at secondhand from an associate for seventy-five cents—and not just any old hat, but one of the dark brown woven-straw type, complete with visor. These dark straws were affected chiefly by the old-timers, and I thus assumed at once a spurious kind of seniority.

A new hand was broken in by spending a week on one route

with a seasoned crew in order to get the hang of things, after which he rode two complete trips with crews on each of the half-dozen or so other lines out of the Olneyville barn. It was my good fortune to be assigned to Conductor Eddie Mann and Motorman Patrick Fitzmaurice. Eddie was a fashion-plate conductor. Not even General Robert E. Lee at the instant of surrender (I omit consideration of the dowdy Grant) could have outsparkled Eddie Mann preparing, at five-fifty A. M., to accept a nickel from a dinner-pail-toting day laborer. Eddie's blue uniform was spotless, and his brass buttons gleamed. His face was always close shaven, his hair always neatly trimmed—I have never known anyone who had a daily haircut, but Eddie always looked as if *he* did. His stiff white collar was always immaculate, and it was authentic linen, not celluloid. His necktie was always in flawless taste and deftly knotted—knotted, too, by Eddie, not ready-knotted and merely hooked on.

Unlike many impeccable dressers, Eddie had no trace of pomposity about him. He was gentle, kindly, crisp and soft of speech. He had a well-timed sense of humor, and laughed often, but always quietly, with a surreptitious sort of chuckle. He never lost his head or his temper. He knew his job, and he knew how to tell me about it. I look back on him as one of the many excellent teachers, whether of English or Greek or transportation, from whom I have, I hope, absorbed some knowledge of mankind.

Pat Fitzmaurice was a mildly harassed giant who wore a black alpaca coat which he always left open, so that the artificial breeze he created in propelling his car kept the coat bellied out on both sides of him, giving him the semblance of an out-size crow in perpetual flight. Later, in off moments at the carbarn, I was often to hear advanced seriously the thesis that the reason so many motormen were fat was because they were always swallowing air.

Since it was summer, the standard car in use was the open, or

"How old is that child?"

bloomer type, as distinguished from the closed, or box, type. We
had two varieties of bloomers on the runs out of Olneyville—
the eight-bench single-truck, hand-braked, and the thirteen-
bench double-truck, hand- and air-braked. Some weeks later,
when the men at the Broad Street carhouse went on a picnic,
several Olneyville crewmen, myself among them, were assigned
to Broad Street for the day, and I had an opportunity to take out
one of the magnificent new fifteen-bench jobs on the Edgewood
and Pawtuxet run. Never before or since have I felt so completely monarch of all I surveyed.

I read the rule book with closer attention than I have ever devoted to any piece of printed matter in my life. While my recollection of it is now somewhat spotty, at the time I knew it virtually by heart. I had to. Knocking down fares (which could
only be accomplished flagrantly, thanks to the fare-collector) or
failure to report an accident would result in instant dismissal.
That seemed reasonable. Yet I have seen car crews deliberately
risk dismissal by neglecting to submit an accident report when
the chances were at least even that the episode would come to
official notice. Why? Simply to avoid an ordeal that terrified
them even more than the prospect of losing their jobs. There are
those who will more readily face charging elephants than attempt to fill out a blank form. I have seen motormen seated at a
table in the carhouse running agonized fingers through their
hair, and gnawing viciously at stubs of unaccustomed pencils, as
they puzzled over the intricacies of DIRECTION CAR WAS
MOVING (no abstruse geodetic computation, but a simple
choice between east and west, which are the only directions railroading knows), NUMBER OF CAR, NAME AND NUM-
BER OF CONDUCTOR, NAME AND NUMBER OF
MOTORMAN, TIME, PLACE, whonot, what not.

The sounding of three bells by the conductor almost invariably foreshadowed the filing of an accident report when the

crew returned to the carhouse. Three bells was the rarely given command for a quick stop. At that signal the motorman shot over his reverse handle and jammed on the air; the car churned to a halt with perhaps only the crew left in their original positions, but the life of some absent-minded or time-pressed soul who was being dragged to a panicky doom might have been saved in the commotion. I have never as a trolley-car passenger heard three bells sounded. In my own rear-platform experience I sounded it three times—once when a youngster jumped at a full ninety-degree angle from a speeding bloomer (he landed on both feet, ran to the curb, and vanished down a side street); once when, in collecting fares along the running board, I saw below me, his head all but touching the rear wheels, a youth who had jumped for the handles and missed them, and who got up and ran away before anything could be done about it; and once when an old man, also jumping for the handles, failed to grasp them and was somehow flung into the center of the tracks behind the car. Thus this last was the only occasion on which the offender obligingly remained for consultation. The motorman and I took possession of him, one by the legs and the other by the shoulders. Through his sparse white hairs a red thread was visible—it seemed a more ominous portent than if he had been dripping gore. We carried him into a clothing store, and a starter and a policeman soon appeared. The starter sent us back to our car, to which we battled our way through a crowd of several hundred of the curious—they probably didn't like to see people get hurt, but if somebody did get hurt they wanted to be there. Never have I known a more nerve-wracking hour than that which followed. Our unfortunate was known neither to the motorman nor to myself, and he had got hurt without our help, but two hearts bled for him more than he was bleeding for himself. When we returned from our run we learned that the thin red trickle across his scalp was an inconsequential scratch which two stitches had already closed (and I hope they hurt a little). He had already signed a statement, the starter told us, declaring that the fault was entirely his own. But, of course, we had to fill out accident reports just the same.

Motormen were required to operate the hand brake exclusively on the first three stops after leaving a terminus, and I never worked with a motorman who did not observe this rule scrupulously. It had been put in the books for the reason that a few years previously an accident which caused several fatalities had apparently been due to the motorman's unfamiliarity with the operation of the hand brake when the air failed to function. During my transportation summer I worked a few trips with a motorman who had been sent to the scene of the catastrophe with a sprinkling car to wash the blood from the road.

The trolleyman was wont to refer to his calling as railroading —to the contempt, I suppose, of the steam railroader. Certainly the romantic advantage must have seemed to the outsider to be with the steam railroader. I am not so sure that it was. The steam railroader, paradoxically, has always been, in a sense, among the most static of mortals. He makes his run and returns home, keeps it up for years, and then retires to a pipe and a bean patch. The representatives of almost any of the trades and most of the professions experience far more variety than he. But the street railroader was emphatically circulatory. Like all men who enjoy their jobs, he was perpetually damning his, but only some fantastic upheaval could blast him out of it. He might fade from sight and none know why or whither he had gone, but he was bound to bob up again in some quarter of the universe on one platform or the other of a trolley car. I remember one Providence motorman whose well-worn uniform carried the brass buttons of the Sacramento Street Railway Company. Those buttons did more than bridge a continent—they were the hallmark of the eternal nomad, defining man as the squirrel in the cage that he is, happy if the patter of his paws can in some degree propitiate his endless craving for motion. I doubt if anyone realized that within a few years practically everyone was going to be his own motorman, and get about all the motion he wanted without arriving anywhere in particular.

" 'Tisn't exactly what it looks like from the sidewalk," an old conductor philosophized after I had been a conductor myself long enough to agree with him. But even after making all due allowance for the insider's vantage-point, street railroading was a mundane, shoulder-rubbing enterprise. It was of the people, by the people, and—despite the oft-repeated, ever-repetitive communications to the press of Only a Passenger—for the people. Apart from some of the lordly suburbans and interurbans, it did not enjoy its own right of way. It lacked the eclecticism and hoity-toityness of the steam railroad. It jostled every variety of horse-drawn and hand-propelled vehicle—the motor car and motor truck had not become the paramount element in the traffic problem, although drivers were already using the car tracks, having not yet learned that a car-track groove raised hob with tires. Passengers and crew could and did pass leisurely time of day with pedestrian friends and acquaintances; the conductor was in continual and essential contact with his fares; the attainment of a front seat on an open car involved utterest proximity to the motorman—one was enjoined, to be sure, from talking to him, but he himself was likely to assume full responsibility for this breach of regulations by opening the conversation.

It was, doubtless, because of its of-the-earth earthiness, its of-the-commonalty commonness, that street-railway transportation was singularly deficient in technical or colorful terminology. I recall only a single instance of trolley jargon that would have been utterly incomprehensible to the outsider. "He throws her around the loop every time he passes Caesar Misch's," said one motorman contemptuously of another. Caesar Misch's was a credit clothing store; the implication was that the maligned motorman was so deeply in this establishment's debt that he always shot by it at full speed, for the loop was the series of notches (from nine to fifteen, depending on the type and the size of the car) on the upper surface of the controller-box over which the controller-handle traveled under the operator's guidance from no power at all to all the power available. One never asked a conductor who his motorman was; one inquired who was on the "front end." The massed passengers constituted a "freight." A "transfer" was not invariably the slip of yellow paper which entitled the passenger to a ride on a different run; around the carbarn it usually meant a car sent out to operate on the time of a scheduled car which had encountered mishap. A "tripper" was an additional but regularly scheduled car (as distinguished from an extra) which ran from a residential to an industrial district in the morning and back again in the evening. A new employee "bucked the list"—took whatever duty was assigned him each morning. No man was likely to be assigned a regular run, in my day, in less than three or four years, and then it would be certain to be a night run. He could hardly hope for a day run for two years more. Some of the more acquisitive among my associates preferred bucking the list to having a regular assignment; in addition to what the office had for them they could usually arrange to substitute for a regular for a trip, or perhaps for half a day, and if substitutes were scarce and the regular wanted time off badly enough, he was often glad to pay the substitute a bonus out of his own pocket. So eager were some of the list-buckers and bonus-seekers that the office had to watch their timecards assiduously to see that they did not violate the ten-hours-in-twelve law.

According to the rule book, the conductor was in charge of the car, but only a seasoned rear-ender with a novice up front was ever likely to attempt to boss his motorman. However composed, however captained, the team generally worked well. My only serious misunderstanding with a motorman arose when I lit a cigarette during a ten-minute layover at a rural terminus. The motorman himself was lighting a pipe when he began to discuss the evils of the cigarette habit, and he was still lighting his pipe nine minutes later, having devoted the interval to withering and obscene invective. Two trips later he was discussing with me his plans for his daughter—she was starting high school in the fall; should she go on to college? She went. I hope she didn't take up cigarettes.

Eddie Mann taught me how to collect fares, how to pull the bell cord, how to handle the problem of children's ages—all the rudimentary essentials that the passenger thought he knew as much about as the conductor did. Therein the passenger erred.

In collecting fares, for example, the conductor depended largely on the automatic honesty of humanity. This was not a moral or ethical quality. It was merely a matter of habit. To present his nickel when the conductor extended his fare-collector was a normal and natural reaction on the part of the passenger. Conductors on regular runs were occasionally confronted with the phenomenon of the habitual would-be fare evader—it was always matter for debate whether he was trying to save money or merely playing a sort of game, as he was usually an old man with not many interests left in life. The policy was to make things miserable for him by jabbing the fare-collector at him every time one passed his seat.

Giving starting and stopping signals might appear to have been an elementary business, but actually there was an art to it. Nothing annoyed a motorman so much as "hard bells." The gong and its little brass clapper were only a couple of feet from his right ear, and hard bells repeated time after time wore down his nervous system. Many a time in later years, as a passenger, I have seen motormen face around savagely and look words they dared not utter in public at a clumsy, hard-bell conductor. When the pair were on the outs about something, a conductor would occasionally give a motorman hard bells deliberately. This made for good feeling all around.

The considerate, skilled conductor soon acquired a technique of signalling that produced a gentle but fully audible *ting* which was almost soothing to the ear. Eddie Mann's bells sounded like tiny carillons.

There was a little game we conductors used to play with the bell cord. An occasional passenger would regard himself as fully capable of ringing his own stop signal. In the case of a habitual offender our procedure was as follows: As the car approached the passenger's stop, the conductor, standing on the back platform, would put his hand to the bell cord and pull it gently taut. This brought the clapper up against the front-end bell without ringing it. When the passenger reached for the bell cord he would yank it, and yank it again, without result. The conductor would be looking somewhere else, and would not notice the passenger until the latter had been carried beyond his stop. The passenger seemed never to discover just what had been put over on him, but he suspected that something had, and thereafter he usually left the operation of the car to the conductor.

If the conductor suspected that a mother was trying to palm off an eight-year-old child on him as an under-fiver, he would keep his fare-collector aimed at her after he had taken her own nickel (the device looked startlingly like a clumsy forty-five). Frequently this would shame her into inserting a second nickel. If she held her ground, and if the conductor was pretty certain that his judgment was accurate, he would inquire, "How old is that child?" in a voice audible to everyone aboard. Few mothers could stand up under that. There was always the chance that if she said, "Four and a half," the tot would cut in with "The hell you say" or something like that.

The running board of an open car had not then become the hazard into which it developed with the growing popularity of the automobile. I recall no near-disasters involving myself, but merely considerable inconvenience when the board was crowded, as it sometimes was, with passengers riding two deep. I once carried ninety-eight fares on a thirteen-bench bloomer capable of seating sixty-five—of the excess, ten or a dozen were squeezed on the back platform; the rest were on the running board. They tried to be helpful, and scrunched back as tightly as they could to let me by in the performance of my duties; even so every passage I made up and down the board involved throwing one arm out around a cluster of humanity and groping blindly for the next handle before letting the first hand loose.

Except on a few long-distance runs, only one of which operated out of Olneyville, a trolley ride in Providence cost a nickel, with a free transfer if the passenger wanted it. Company executives had passes, and fellow-motormen and conductors rode on their hats. The longest local run, to Buttonwoods, down Narragansett Bay, operated out of the Broad Street carhouse. It employed a special type of closed car, with sidewise seats like a railroad coach, and for a good part of the distance it had its own right of way. To my unsophisticated eye the Buttonwoods car had all the pomp and splendor of the Gilt Edge Express from Boston to New York. You had to pay twenty cents to go from downtown Providence to Buttonwoods, but such a magnificent journey was worth every cent of it.

A company rule specified that a conductor must start work with five dollars' worth of change in his pockets. In practice most conductors started with about two dollars' worth. I once had the foolhardiness to initiate operations with exactly three nickels. Of my first three passengers, one proffered a nickel and each of the next two a dollar bill. They rode free. Had one of them been a representative of the company I should, I hope, have been dismissed as soon as word of my inadequacy was reported.

Drunken passengers were an occasional nuisance. If the conductor were on the alert, he could sometimes prevent drunks from becoming passengers, but sometimes they slipped aboard. The motion of the car, combined perhaps with the brassy stench that seemed to be peculiar to trolleys, frequently made them sick. In that case there was nothing for it but to put them off—a business for which I usually enlisted the help of the motorman, for they were fragile charges, and we did not want anything to happen to them as long as they were under our jurisdiction. We would guide the offender to the sidewalk and deposit him gently on the curb, with his back against a telephone pole, and leave him there to ponder the perils of excessive indulgence. I recall no drunk who was even slightly combative—perhaps they just didn't feel up to it. The mess that remained behind I would attend to in this wise: Every car had a sand container on each platform, and the motorman would draw on this supply if the tracks were slippery and he couldn't get traction. I would get a scoopful or two of sand and scatter it over the mess. This concealed it effectively, and after two or three trips no trace of it was likely to remain. There was no room on the car for a brush and a pail of water anyway.

Just as every railroad train has a number, so did every trolley run have a special identifying designation. If a line operated on a fifteen-minute headway and a round trip took an hour and a quarter, five cars and ten crews were required to maintain its full daily schedule. The first car to leave the barn at five o'clock every morning on the Plainfield Street run, for instance, would be designated the first Plainfield Street, and it would be followed, at quarter-hour intervals, by the second, third, fourth, and fifth Plainfield Streets. At eleven-thirty every morning a night crew would relieve the day crew of the first Plainfield Street, which thereby became the sixth Plainfield Street. The first's crew would go to lunch (perhaps riding home on what had been their own car) and would take the car back an hour and a quarter (one round trip) later, at which time it would revert to its original status of first Plainfield Street. The night crew would take over again at five o'clock, and the first Plainfield Street once again became the sixth and continued the sixth until it completed its day's run (a total of eighteen and a half hours' service) at eleven-thirty that night. The seventh, eighth, ninth, and tenth Plainfield Streets, themselves metamorphosed out of the second, third, fourth, and fifth, followed it into the barn at fifteen-minute intervals, and the line was locked up for the night. I do not cite these as precise timetable figures, but they will give the idea. As I recall it, only the Westminster Street run, going down into the heart of Providence and back to Olneyville Square, operated all night.

Providence enjoyed one street-railway eccentricity which was, I believe, peculiar to itself. This was the College Hill cable car. There have been plenty of cable systems, but this was purely an auxiliary, an accessory device. College Hill in Providence—now, alas, trackless (they dug a tunnel under Waterman Street)—is one of the steepest gradients in America which is still a regularly used street. At the foot of the hill, in my time, a streetcar was hitched to a tiny car which gripped an underground cable. The cable-car motorman (there was just room in his apparatus for himself and a coupling boy) pulled a lever which closed the grip on the cable, and the whole business rolled up the hill together, the passenger car in advance. At the top of the hill the cable car cut loose and the passenger car shot ahead under its own power. The process was reversed going down—the cable car, hitched in front of the passenger car, now acted as a brake, for while the passenger car could easily have coasted down, it might have coasted a little too easily and bounced half-way to the other side of town if things had kept out of its way.

Only the little eight-bench single-truck cars were used on the hill, and these were all hand-braked.

There was only one drawback to this arrangement from the point of view of the crew of the passenger car, particularly the conductor's. College Hill was double-tracked, and there were two cable cars, one for each track. A passenger car going up or down took whichever cable car was available. The odds were even whether you were to draw the right-hand or the left-hand track. If you got the left-hand, you had to fold up the right-hand running board, let down the left-hand running board, and put up the left-hand side bar out of the way. At the end of the trip, whether up or down, you had to put everything back where it belonged. You could take a chance and leave both side bars down and the left-hand running board up, but in that case some dear little old lady would want to get off at Benefit Street, the only stop on the Hill, and you had to make the laborious transformation anyway. At the top of the Hill you would let down the right-hand running board, and, if you were really expert, hook up the left-hand running board while the car was in motion.

On my sixty-third consecutive and final day as a conductor (I worked exactly nine weeks in a row, Fourth of July and Labor Day and Sundays included), I had a run that took me up College Hill, and on my last trip up we drew the left-hand track. A passenger gave me a dollar bill which I had not yet had time to change. (It was always a good idea to hold onto a bill for a time anyway—it kept the passenger anxious, and thereafter he would probably think twice before he gave a conductor big money in payment of a five-cent fare.) I stuck the bill in the outside breast pocket of my coat. In the flurry of picking up the running board on the fly, the bill apparently fell out of the pocket. I gave the passenger his ninety-five cents' change and I also gave him loud-voiced hell for daring to give a conductor a dollar bill. I would be through railroading forever in about fifty minutes and I had nothing to lose. I very nearly got my dollar's worth out of the satisfaction I derived from this incident. I only hope the passenger wrote a letter to the company and asked that stern measures be taken with Conductor 642.

Conductors did not have to know anything about electricity. Neither, for that matter, did motormen. When the low-priced automobile came in and an occasional trolleyman bought one to take him to and from the carhouse, I am sure he speedily acquired a deeper awareness of the workings of his motor car than he ever had of the workings of a trolley car. Every trolley car had a circuit breaker tucked under the platform roof at each end, and when the current load became too heavy (at least I suppose that was the explanation) the front-end circuit breaker would snap off with a crash and a sheet of blue flame, scaring the wits out of the passengers and setting children crying. The motorman would reach up and throw the handle back, and all was well.

The circuit breaker was a boxlike device which was suspended on little pegs about an inch below the roof of the car, and the resulting pocket made an admirable repository for the long wallet which every conductor carried (it was a little too bulky to fit an inside coat pocket) and in which he kept collected transfers, witness slips, day card, and other essential documents. I was reaching up one day to tuck my wallet into this convenient receptacle when I felt a tremendous thump in the middle of the back—the sort Jack Johnson might have given me. Looking around to see who had taken this unwarranted liberty, I found myself alone on the platform. Then I realized what had happened. In sticking my fingers into the slot in the circuit breaker I had touched the main cable and received the full current that propelled the car. Thereafter I approached the circuit breaker with daintiness and delicacy.

The only mechanical defect that developed in any of the cars I rode that summer was a fracture of the trolley wheel. It broke cleanly into two parts—two thinner wheels—right through the center of the flanges which held it to the wire. We were about two miles from the terminus at Hunt's Mills, and during the rest of the trip I had to hold the trolley rope so that one piece of the wheel was in contact with the overhead wire. It was a pretty rough contact, and the sparks that popped in an endless shower, giving our progression the effect of a horizontal skyrocket, provided me with more than enough light to see what I was about. When we reached Hunt's Mills I called the carhouse, and a car-tink came out with a new trolley wheel. Car-tinks were the men who made routine repairs around the barn or out on a run. If a car required more radical overhauling it was run or towed to the big repair shops just over the city line on Cranston Street.

Even without splitting in half, the trolley wheel occasionally jumped the wire in spite of its deep flanges. Then it was the conductor's job to get it back on again, which was no trouble in the daytime, but took a few minutes longer on a country road on a cloudy and moonless night. So far as I can recall, no one yanked the trolley off out of mischief on any of my cars—it was summer, and there were no football victories to celebrate.

Outside of his handles—controller, reverse, and air—the only piece of equipment which a motorman had to use was the switch-bar. This was a long steel rod, similar to a stoker's slice-bar, with a flattened end which the motorman inserted into a switch, turning the frog by twisting the bar to left or right. If a switch were obstinate he would have to get off the car and pry it loose, and naturally this annoyed him. At busy intersections, such as Dorrance and Westminster Streets, a worker was usually stationed to relieve motormen of this chore (and to save valuable time) during rush hours. I think Providence already had a few automatic switches at that time—these turned if the motorman applied a notch of power. Later they became universal. The switch-bar was indispensable if a car left the track, provided at least one wheel remained no farther away from one rail than the length of the switch-bar itself. My trolley experience included a single jump. We hit a facing switch point at a turnout a little faster than we ought to have. Our front wheels went off the rails. The motorman got down, put one end of the switch-bar against a truck wheel and the other on the rail, got back on his platform, and applied power. We sailed squarely back onto the rails. Conductors found the switch-bar useful in turning the direction signs on the fronts and sides of cars. Altogether the switch-bar was an indispensable piece of equipment—like a bayonet, you could do everything with it but sit on it.

The only occasion on which I had the handles in my own hands was at the end of a run one midnight after we had dropped our last passenger. My motorman and I had been together for nearly three weeks (this was my longest stretch all that summer on a single run), and had I remained in the street-car business I should have asked for no finer partner. (Yes, I remember his name, but I shall not disclose it—he may still be on the payroll.) I asked him right out if he would let me take the car. "Sure," he said. I drove for perhaps a quarter of a mile, but it was one of the big thrills of my life, and I just missed a magnificent climax by rattling into a turnout at a speed that almost threw us off the rails.

Breaking in a motorman was a more involved procedure, for teacher and pupil alike, than breaking in a conductor. The instructor, if he wanted to (and some did), could make the business exceedingly trying for the novitiate. I recall one grizzled old tutor who would invariably say to a newcomer on his first training trip: "Step over there out of the way. Just watch me and don't say anything. Them's rules." Then, presumably to demonstrate that a veteran was not obliged to worry his head over rules, he would open up a protracted conversation with a front-seat passenger. Two days later, having ignored his charge completely in the interval, the old fellow would suddenly throw his controller-handle around the loop, jump to one side, and yell, "Take her!" It was something like teaching a youngster to swim by shoving him off the end of a wharf. The student would clutch the handles and then, usually, bring the car to a sudden and shattering stop. He was always a little afraid (and properly so) of the power he held in his hands; he would invariably crowd on too much air, and as a result the compressors under the car floor were perpetually athrob in an effort to keep up with him. Some motormen never learned how to operate a car properly; others developed into artists endowed with the competence and adroitness of the skipper of a racing sloop.

But to return to my own course of training. It was Eddie Mann who taught me to call streets. This may sound like a highly rudimentary form of instruction. I grant that. Let us say rather that it was Eddie Mann who instilled in me the courage to call streets.

For some reason I was in a mild state of panic at the prospect. I had taken a course in public speaking at college. I still do not know why I chose it, but I would not have missed it for the world, for it provided the most hilarious and enjoyable moments of my entire educational process—as long, that is, as some other student was speaking. Every few days each of us was called upon to make a three-minute address on any subject he wished. The addresses were lame and halting things, and were accompanied by ridiculous mechanical gestures; moreover, instead of roaring up to a climax, they merely dribbled away into silence—a silence invariably broken by the ironic applause of the class and of Professor Thomas Crosby.

These occasions had been painful enough, but at least the speaker's audience had been facing him, as an audience should.

But to bellow the names of streets at the necks of a carload of passengers seemed different. I felt as if I could easily have gone to the front platform and announced: "Ladies and gentlemen, may I have your attention for a moment, please. We are now approaching Barton Street."

"Time you began calling streets," said Eddie one afternoon as we were rolling up Broadway with a fair-sized freight of homeward-bound shoppers. "Go ahead—next one is Dean."

"Dean Street," I whispered in the strictest confidence to the roof of the car.

"I beg your pardon?" inquired Eddie, cupping his right hand behind his ear. "Are you trying to keep it secret? Come on, now —next is Ringgold."

"Ringgold Street," I reported conversationally to a point in midair halfway up the car.

"Look," said Eddie. "We're supposed to get rid of this freight by the time we reach Olneyville Square. Give 'em a little encouragement. Next is Pallas."

"Pallas Street," I told an old man who was dozing on the rear bench. He dozed on.

"Yell it," said Eddie. "Yell it like hell. They pay you to do it. Come on now—Battey Street."

I closed my eyes and roared "Battey Street!" Then I opened them. A woman turned and signalled me as if I had reminded her of something. That was all. I gave Pat Fitzmaurice a bell and the passenger alighted. Thereafter, as fast as I learned them, I bellowed street names along whatever route I was operating, with zest and gusto.

I already knew Providence and its environs pretty well, but there were still parts of the surrounding area that had been undiscovered country until I ventured into them as a conductor. One afternoon, in a Rumford-bound car, we were waiting for the cable car to haul us up College Hill when a woman on the sidewalk asked me: "Do you pass the Wannamoisett Country Club?"

"No, ma'am," I said with finality.

"Yes, you do," proclaimed a male passenger with somewhat more incisive finality.

This was the most embarrassing incident of my entire transportation career.

I spent a week with Eddie and Pat by way of getting my basic training. Thereafter I put in two trips on each of the other lines running out of the Olneyville carhouse. Most of the routes were double-tracked, but the tail-ends of a few that ran out into the country were single-tracked. The Dyer Avenue–Swan Point run was one of these on the Dyer Avenue end.

I picked up the Dyer Avenue car to which I was assigned for two trips one afternoon in Olneyville Square. It was just as well that my training was well advanced by this time, because the regular conductor paid me little notice. He had other things on his mind. He was in the middle of a quarrel with his motorman, and the row was being conducted loudly over the heads of the delighted passengers.

Before we reached the end of the line, out near the Cranston Print Works, I was able to piece the story together. On the previous trip the car had stalled on a stretch of track where a shower had washed a thin layer of gravel over the rails. The current could not get through to the ground. The predicament was neither uncommon nor desperate. When it occurred, the conductor's job was to take the switch-bar, scrape the gravel away from the rail as closely as possible to the point where the wheel touched the rail, and hold the switch-bar so that it was in contact with both the wheel and the bit of exposed rail. The motorman then applied a notch of power; the current ran through the wheel and the switch-bar into the rail, and the car rolled forward to clean track.

The conductor had to take care, however, to touch the switch-bar to the rail first, and then slide it along until it contacted the wheel. If he touched the wheel first, and if the motorman threw on a notch of power at the same time, the current would go to ground through the conductor (who would thereby become, quite literally, a conductor). A notch of power wasn't much, but, after all, it *was* electricity. It might sting the conductor's hands, or it might, if the ground were wet, fling him clear across the road.

My conductor had got just such a hand-sting, plus a pride-sting that irked him much more. Out of the charges and counter-charges that flew back and forth across the benches I became convinced that both parties were at fault—that the conductor had touched the wheel first but was damned if he would admit it, and that before he could ground the switch-bar the motorman had applied power and was damned if *he* would admit it.

We reached the end of the line and discharged our last glee-ful passengers. I was a little apprehensive as to what might happen now. Freed of the inhibitions imposed by the presence of the traveling public, and on solid earth instead of aboard the bouncing little eight-bencher (which was hardly a practicable arena), would they fly at each other hammer and tongs—or controller-handle and fare-collector, each potentially a formidable weapon? Happily they did not. With the departure of the passengers they sparked up their vocabularies a little, but nothing worse. Even this did not last long, for a stout housewife carrying a shopping bag of black netting climbed onto the car, followed by a couple of hands from the print works, and the recriminations thereupon settled back to the monotonous give-and-take of insult minus profanity.

We started back toward town. There were few stops—it was after five, and travel now would be almost entirely in the opposite direction. This comparative leisure gave the crew plenty of opportunity to keep their invective flowing back and forth. The new crop of passengers enjoyed it for a while, but I was heartily sick of it, and looked forward without pleasure to the remainder of my two trips on the Dyer Avenue run. Moreover, I could not see that I was advancing my knowledge of my profession. In this respect, the event proved, I was greatly in error.

The Dyer Avenue line was single-tracked from the Cranston Print Works terminus down to the junction with Plainfield Street. A mile from the terminus was a double-tracked turnout where two cars could pass each other. Arrived at the turnout, the motorman of an in-bound car threw off the light which had protected him on the way in from the terminus, and which would have held any out-bound car in the turnout. Then, if the light covering the stretch from the turnout to Plainfield Street was out (indicating a clear track), the motorman threw it on, thereby protecting the run down to the Plainfield Street junction.

The signal lights were small incandescent bulbs which glowed pallidly if the sun was shining, but which were visible enough for the purpose they served. The motorman threw a light by inserting the end of his reverse-handle into a socket-switch—a device intended to prevent any mischievously inclined person from tampering with it.

With the stopping of the car at the turnout the quarrel grew louder, or seemed to in the sudden silence. Even the passengers were no longer amused. The motorman stepped back on the front end, and the conductor gave him two viciously hard bells; the motorman threw the handle venomously around the loop, jerking everybody's head back, and we banged out of the turnout onto the final stretch of single track.

At Laurel Hill Avenue the right of way curved with the highway in a broad, easy sweep. Around the curve appeared a streetcar, the twin of our own, full of homeward-bound passengers. There was no actual danger, for there was plenty of room for each car to stop in, but still it didn't look like the ideal way to operate a street-railway system.

A subdued conductor and motorman got down for a brief conference with the crew of the outbound car. The Plainfield Street junction was only a couple of hundred yards ahead, so the outbound car changed ends and ran down to the junction, with the passengers looking a little silly all riding backward, but apparently enjoying the novelty of the situation. We trailed along behind. At the junction, the outbound car ran up the Plainfield Street tracks far enough to let us by, and we ran into town on a foolproof pair of rails and, apart from the rattle of the car, in the midst of an exhilarating silence.

When I reported to the carhouse for assignment the following day I was ordered to the superintendent's office and faced that dignitary for the first time since I had reported for duty some ten days earlier. If I thought he was going to press me for details of the previous day's incident I was wrong—he had all the details he needed.

"You want to watch those lights," he said. "It's the conductor's job as much as it is the motorman's. You've read the rules, and you know that. You can guess how serious that thing might have been yesterday if the Laurel Hill Avenue curve had been a little sharper. It's a serious enough thing anyway just to have us all look like a pack of damn fools, getting hung up like that between lights. That crew has earned a five-day layoff for themselves. Maybe it'll learn 'em not to do their fighting in public. Now you, as third man on the car, were just as responsible for what happened as either of the others. You're new, and this'll be a lesson to you. It better be. All you're getting is this bawling out."

That evening I read the rule book through again. I thought it would be a good idea to be prepared for every possible contingency. I figured there was one contingency I should never again have to worry about. That was my mistake.

XVI

A Special Kind of Insult

ONE aspect of my new calling was a continuing exasperation—and so it was to everyone who took a car out of Olneyville carhouse or any other, in Providence or in any other community where trolley cars ran. This was the employment of "spotters," as the laity called them—we knew them as "suckers," a designation invariably qualified with a series of adjectives or adjectival phrases. For example, I would report for my equipment at the carhouse office and be told: "On such-and-such a trip last Thursday you registered thirty-seven fares. Should have been thirty-eight. Watch it." A sucker had turned me in. No proof whatever that the sucker was right—it was my count against his. Or hers.

No one of us had the slightest idea who the suckers were. I doubt if the carhouse office knew. Some of them were reputedly motormen and conductors themselves, functioning both on the road and in the carhouse, for it was as simple a matter to shatter a regulation right in the carhouse as anywhere else—neglecting to set the hand brake, leaving the headlight on, failing to turn off the air-compressor. I know that as a newcomer, and a newcomer fresh from college, I was at first looked upon with general distrust. It took a few mutual breaches of trolley law to establish my *bona fides;* the grapevine quickly carried the good news to all concerned, and I was accepted into the fraternity of the sinned-against non-sinning.

Soon after I finished breaking in, a new conductor whom I

remember only as Bill was assigned to the Olneyville carhouse. There had been a few new hands in between, but Bill stands out in my memory for the reason that the finger of suspicion became pointed at him a day or two after he came among us. Motormen and conductors were always just as credulous as anybody else. A car-tink came running into the locker room late one afternoon and announced to the perpetual pinochle game that he had found Bill lying down on one of the long felt-covered benches in an old-fashioned closed car with seats that ran lengthwise. Bill had seemed to be sound asleep at the moment of discovery, and therefore, if he was spotting, was recreant to his trust. But the pinochle players agreed with the car-tink that, asleep or awake, Bill had been up to no good, though just what errors of commission or of omission he might have been capable of observing, even with binoculars, from the gloomy interior of a closed car parked in a remote corner of the shed were not specified.

When Bill came into the locker room, yawning and rubbing one eye with a knuckle, he was greeted with silence and frosty stares. I was waiting for the next day's list to be posted. Bill came over and sat down beside me on a bench under the windows. I felt somewhat as if a leper were climbing into bed with me. Still I was determined not to join in the already functioning program to send Bill to Coventry—certainly not until further and more substantial returns were in. Bill was a silent, stolid sort who looked too stupid to be good sucker material. But, there again, you couldn't tell—that may have been just the kind the company wanted. And perhaps Bill merely looked stupid but wasn't.

Bill made himself a cigarette and borrowed a match from me, not forgetting to return the book. I asked him what run he had had that day. He told me he had been running up and down Plainfield Street since five-thirty that morning, and considering that he had worked until twelve-thirty the previous night he was about ready to stumble home and fall into bed as soon as the list was posted.

A few minutes later the list went up, and Bill and I found that we were both down for five-o'clock reports the following morning. Bill went out, and forthwith the pinochle players became as vocal as crows. There were a couple named Charlie and Jim, usually the life of the party, who were particularly bitter. Jim, it appeared, had been turned in for short fares three times recently, and was suspicious of the whole human race above the age of four.

Bill and I and the other five-o'clocks were on hand in good season the following morning along with the regular day crews. A street-railway barn at five A. M. was invariably a panorama of pandemonium. Out in the carshed the day foreman was getting the crews on the platforms at some peril to his well-being, since cars were darting at him from half a dozen tracks at once. In the doorway of the locker room stood the assistant superintendent, carbook in hand, announcing assignments in a roar optimistically designed to carry above the general hubbub: "Delaney! Oh, Delaney! Seen Delaney? Hey, you five-o'clocks—Bechhofer, Hanson, Dawley—you Dawley—get on the third Hartford Avenue with Salzman—car five seven eight! Hurry, boy—you're due at the hose-house turnout already! Bechhofer, take the ninth tripper—car eight six three—Bateman's on front. Run along, boy—time you wasn't here! Eight six three, I told you! She does like hell brake hard, Bateman—that's just your God-damned imagination!"

Punctual and punctilious motormen who had whole seconds to spare were fumbling in their lockers, debating the prospects of rain and whether or not to take their oilskins. Conductors were lined up at the office window getting their day cards; they snatched up their equipment and dashed to their platforms, while fuming motormen who had no truck with paperwork

His fingers dripped a yellow, viscous liquid.

gonged angrily for bells. And throughout the din, old George the janitor, stoop-shouldered and bowlegged, ran his long-handled broom sketchily under the locker-room benches and squinted into empty cigarette boxes for treasure-trove in the shape of coupons.

Bill had got his stuff and was sticking a bunch of transfer pads into an inside breast pocket when Charlie, fooling with Jim, gave Jim a shove which knocked him against Bill. Bill was heavy, and solid on his feet, but the jolt was powerful enough to cause him to take a hasty step backward to preserve his balance.

"Take it easy, you yaps," he cautioned.

Bill planned to make street-railway transportation his life-work. Although by the rules he wouldn't be required to wear one until he had been with the company three months, he already had a brand-new uniform, complete with change pockets which were protected against wear by shiny leather guards. In the manner of an old hand, he had formed the habit of keeping his fingers in these pockets, with the thumbs left outside. He assumed this pose quite naturally when he had tucked his transfer-pads away, and as he did so I saw a sharp, alert, wholly uncharacteristic glint in his usually expressionless eyes. Then a crimson glow rose up around the curve of his chin and spread rapidly up his cheeks.

He pulled his fingers out of his right-hand pocket. They dripped a yellow, viscous liquid that was all too readily identifiable as the yolk of an overripe egg.

Charlie and Jim were still at their buffoonery, which at the moment consisted of elaborate shadowboxing, with an exhibition of what Jim obviously intended to be superior footwork.

"Hey, you two!" bellowed Bill.

Charlie and Jim stopped their fooling and stared at him.

"What's eatin' *you?*" asked Jim; then, catching sight of the dripping fingers, "Well, for the love of Mike!"

"I don't know which one of you two is to blame for this," said Bill in a quiet voice that had all the brittleness of an icicle, "but I allow to find out. And when I do find out I'll do somethin' about it."

He walked to the washroom. A dozen or so early-report men had seen the thing, and by nightfall, of course, every man in the Olneyville carhouse would know about it. It was several minutes before Bill came out of the washroom. After all, it had taken some time to get that pocket in working order again, and besides that he had had to wash each individual nickel. There was a big wet patch around the edge of the pocket, and there were a few flakes of toilet paper that could not be brushed off until the patch was dry.

During the next two weeks there were no fresh developments in the situation. Motormen who teamed with Bill were not turned in, and the idea began to take hold that perhaps, after all, he was just another conductor. I don't know whether Charlie and Jim made a special point of keeping out of Bill's way, but at least their paths did not cross in my presence.

The crossing of the paths, when it did come about, was under Bill's personal management. It was late in the afternoon, and the day conductors were turning in their cash and their cards. The eternal pinochle game was in full cry, with Charlie and Jim among the melders.

Bill came into the locker room and walked over to the pinochle game and hung a scruffy dead chicken, suspended from a loop of clothesline, around Charlie's neck. Charlie reached up his hands, as anybody would naturally in those circumstances, but Bill batted the hands down.

"Leave that alone," he said, "or I'll nail it to you."

Charlie was stiff with fright, but again, involuntarily, his hands went up—people don't like ropes around their necks, with or without dead chickens attached.

"I said leave that alone," said Bill, "or I'll nail it to you. Boys," and Bill turned to the crowd that had gathered, "I don't know for sure if this rat's a sucker, but he prob'ly is. It runs in the family."

"What do you mean?" somebody asked.

"What I mean is this. I been turned in for short fares two or three times. I didn't like it. I allowed I'd find out who was doin' it. I begun to look over the freights I was carryin'. I noticed a little old man was ridin' with me pretty often on a late afternoon in-trip when things are light—I guess this dude can't count very high. He didn't read a paper and he didn't watch the scenery and he seemed to turn his head around a lot. So I missed a couple of fares on purpose, and couple days later the office tells me I missed *three*. I know it ain't so, but I know, too, by now that this dude is a sucker all right. I rode that same car yesterday as a passenger, and the dude was there. He gets off downtown and I gets off. He goes into a bank and up to a counter and writes somethin' in a little book he took out of his pocket, and then he goes out—he don't put any money in or take any out like an honest person would do if they went into a bank. I followed him and he took a Plainfield Street home. So did I. He got off at Webster Avenue and walked south and let himself into the upper tenement of a two-family house. I rang the downstairs doorbell and a woman came and I made out I was takin' a church census and was they Baptists or what. I ask her about the other family in the house and by jiminy, the old dude is"—he grabbed Charlie's shoulder and shook it—"is this rat's old man. The old man used to work in a bank himself, on'y now he's on a pension or somethin', and he makes his tobacco money bein' a sucker. Like father, like son, they always say. And if you're a sucker yourself, a good way to cover it up is to get people thinkin' some other feller is."

Charlie cowered in his chair. He had made no further move to get rid of the chicken.

"That ain't so," said Charlie in a low, dead voice. "What my old man does is his business. Anybody says I'm a sucker is—"

"Say that word and I'll ram that hen down your throat. Beat it— beat it before I knock the livin' spit out o' you."

Charlie beat it.

A month or so later I asked Bill if he had seen the old man since the chicken incident.

"Nope," he grinned. "He's been fired."

"Fired? How do you know?"

"Well, I don't *know,* if you mean really knowin' it. But I'd bet a million dollars on it. I fixed it so he *would* be fired."

"How?"

"Look—I'm tellin' this to you and to nobody else. Remember me sayin' that that dude couldn't count high numbers? Well, I'd thought that up earlier as a special kind of insult, him bein' a banker and all. Then I figured, suppose I made it true. Suppose I fix it so it looks like he really can't count. So every trip he rides with me I slip in four or five extra nickels. See? If *we're* short a couple fares *we* catch hell, and if we keep on bein' short we're fired. Well, suppose a sucker begins bein' short on *his* count, and then he's short four or five fares a few times, don't you suppose they tell him he can't count and finally fire him? Should ought to work both ways, shouldn't it? It's a cinch it does. I'd certainly fire a guy like that if *I* owned the company. Wouldn't you?"

I said I would.

"What was the idea of that dead chicken stuff?" I asked.

"I guess I got bankin' on the brain," Bill chuckled. "I just wanted to give that rat a little int'rest on his egg."

XVII

The Redemption of Peleg Champlin

ONE warm midsummer night during my brief career as a trolley-car conductor I was sitting on the rear bench of my car on a turnout not far from the Charles Street terminus of the Hartford Avenue–Charles Street line. The car was a thirteen-bench open type, and the seat I was occupying faced back in the direction we had come. The view was not spectacular—a huge, silent, unillumined cotton mill, and beside it, reaching almost up to the tracks, a marshy expanse overgrown with tall, swordlike rushes that stretched away into the darkness. The air was limpid and pleasant; crickets and locusts were chanting soothing nocturnes; the hard bench was agreeably restful after several hours of standing on the back platform and walking up and down the running board collecting fares. This was the last trip out—in another forty minutes we would be rolling into the barn and calling it a day.

I have no idea who my motorman was. If he was Fred Bishop, as he well may have been, the situation was fraught with unrealized drama that was not to reach its first bloody climax for three years; and there would be more to follow. For if he was Bishop, then within the next few seconds a murderer and his victim were within a car-length or less of each other, with neither aware of what the future held in store.

As I say, the motorman could have been Fred Bishop. I made several trips with him, and it is possible that on one of them he and the other were even closer together than a car-length—we might even have carried the other as a passenger, in which capacity he would almost certainly have ridden on the front seat, at the motorman's elbow, or even have stood beside him, which he had the authority to do. Bishop was a tall, stoop-shouldered, stolid, plodding man—a mildly Lincolnian figure—with tousselled dark brown hair and a sweeping brown mustache. He spoke seldom, and then softly. It was difficult to imagine him losing his temper. He was a good motorman, and it was pleasant to work with him, even though layovers at terminals were usually devoid of conversation. I remember that on one Sunday trip Bishop had a friend along with him for the ride, on the front seat, and as a courtesy to Bishop I declined to accept the gentleman's nickel—a courtesy, by the way, in which the company would have declined to back me up.

The crickets and locusts chanted on. Above their song I could hear in the distance the hum of the inbound car that was to pass us on the turnout. It reached the turnout, clattered over the switch points, stopped. The two motormen got down off their platforms and walked over to the signal lights and clicked them, the one off, the other on. I could hear the clicks. My car rocked gently as my motorman climbed back aboard. Only then did I get up off the rear bench and prepare to give him his starting signal.

Out of the rushes at the side of the road stepped a uniformed figure. It was almost as if he had been hiding there, or perhaps he had crossed the marsh by a path I had not noticed, and which the rushes concealed. He was Inspector Peleg Champlin—short, alert, always immaculately garbed. He had a small, neatly trimmed gray mustache. He was not unpopular as inspectors go. Certainly he was not unpopular with the company, for he was always strictly on the job. He was certainly on the job now.

"You want to watch those signal lights," he cautioned me.

"You're just as responsible for them as the motorman is, you know."

I knew. All I could do was to nod in agreement. Inspector Champlin boarded the inbound car and was whisked away. Next day when I reported for work I was laid off one trip for failing to watch my motorman throw signal lights. I bore Inspector Champlin no grudge. He had done his duty—I had not done mine. This combination of circumstances cost me about forty cents' pay.

During the few remaining weeks of my career as a trolley-car conductor I probably saw Inspector Champlin half a dozen times, usually in Olneyville Square, where most crew changes were made, and where he had a curbstone telephone connected with the carhouse. We always passed the time of day not uncordially.

Three years went by before Champlin made the headlines. That was in 1915. He made them again (and the conservative *Providence Journal* had never used bigger) in 1930. No longer living, he continued to make them off and on for fifteen years more. Officially, Champlin did not cease to be news until 1945. But his story has taken so many fantastic twists in the course of a generation that no one would have the temerity to say that "finis" has yet been written to it. It began with a murder—a crude, clumsy, brutal, messy, sordid, readily solvable murder. Since I was no longer a resident of Providence at the time, and never saw either Bishop or Champlin again after the summer of 1912, I shall tell the story objectively, since it touches me only in the detail of my casual acquaintance with the principals. But not everyone has been acquainted even casually with both a murderer and his victim.

A doctor named Streker—W. S. Streker—occupied the second floor, over Corrigan's drugstore, of the wooden apartment build-

The door of the Bishop kitchen was still open.

ing at the corner of Westminster and Messer Streets in Providence. On the morning of November 21, 1915, a raw, blustery, squally morning, Dr. Streker was awakened by a noise which he later described as "like that of a man falling to the floor." It came, apparently, from the apartment above him. Dr. Streker struck a match, lighted the gas jet, and looked at his watch. Four o'clock. He thought, too, that he heard a click as though someone had closed a door. He opened a window, stuck out his head, and looked up and down Messer Street. No one was in sight. Dr. Streker went back to bed.

Two and a half hours later, Catherine Mullaley, Dr. Streker's maid, who slept on the fourth floor, got up and dressed and went down the rear stairway to the Streker apartment. She noticed that the kitchen door leading into the third-floor apartment was open. That apartment, she knew, was occupied by a motorman named Bishop, his wife, and two men roomers. Catherine gave the matter no further thought, but went about her household duties. Around one o'clock she started up to her fourth-floor room. The door of the Bishop kitchen was still open. What was more unusual, the shades were drawn—a detail she could easily have failed to notice when she had come down to work in the dawn of a gray November day.

She went back to the Streker apartment and told the doctor about the open door and the drawn shades. The doctor recalled the thump he had heard at four o'clock. He went down to the drugstore and told the proprietor, M. R. Corrigan, who also owned the building. The two men walked up the back stairway to the third floor and were about to enter the kitchen when they stopped in their tracks. The doorknob was stained with blood. They tiptoed inside. There was more blood on the inner knob and on the key, which was in the lock. They crossed the kitchen to the living room and looked in.

On the floor, face down, clad in a nightshirt, lay Bishop's gory and battered body. The feet were just over the threshold of the bedroom. The left side of the head was cut and hacked in half a dozen places. Both nightshirt and carpet were saturated with blood, and blood was spattered as high up as six feet on the walls of the room. Streker saw there was nothing he could do. Corrigan hurried back to the drugstore and telephoned the police.

It was apparent to the police that Bishop had first been attacked in bed (there was blood on the pillow but not on the sheets) and that he had then fought his way across the bedroom into the living room, where he had been shot four times. A little later, when the two roomers were questioned (one of them was a streetcar conductor), they said they had heard no shots and had not been awakened by the struggle. This, the medical examiner subsequently explained, was because the weapon had been jammed against Bishop and the discharges had "fairly exploded within the body"—a technique which had the effect of deadening the reports "as would a mechanical silencer." On the floor of the bedroom the police found a revolver holster and a police constable's nickel-plated badge.

Naturally the police wondered where Mrs. Bishop was. She turned up at the apartment around six o'clock that evening. She said she had spent the previous night with a Mr. and Mrs. Long in Pawtucket, and this was confirmed. But the police had an idea that Mrs. Bishop might still have some important constructive information, and they went after it. After several hours' questioning by two inspectors she admitted intimacies with Inspector Peleg E. Champlin of the Rhode Island Company extending back over a two-year period. Champlin had a key to the back door of the Bishop apartment. As an authority on local transit schedules he knew, of course, precisely where Bishop was at any minute of his working day. Mrs. Bishop identified the badge and holster as Champlin's property. He had once been a constable in the neighboring town of Johnston, and apparently carried the badge with him as a pocket-piece.

Champlin was picked up while the questioning of Mrs. Bishop was in progress. The police found him in his room at a house on Central Street. By one o'clock the following morning they had a complete, written confession.

Champlin had gone to the apartment, he declared, "as per agreement with F. H. Bishop." He rapped twice at the kitchen door before Bishop called "Who's there?" "Champ," answered Champlin. (Later he quoted Mrs. Bishop as addressing him by his middle name of Everett. Apparently if one has been christened Peleg, one prefers to be called anything else.)

Bishop, in his nightgown, had led the way to the bedroom, indicated the edge of the bed, and said, "Sit down." Then came this dialogue:

Bishop: "Have you seen Leah [Mrs. Bishop] today?"

Champlin: "No."

Bishop: "Have you seen Leah today?"

Champlin: "No."

Bishop then called Champlin a liar and "struck at" him. (Had Champlin obeyed Bishop's order to sit down? Was Bishop standing?) Champlin's confession continued:

"He missed me, but clutched me by the throat. I went over backwards on the bed. I then hit him with a blackjack. When I struck him with the blackjack he released his hold on my throat. I arose from the bed, and he struck at me again. He threw me on the floor, and as I thought he was getting the best of me I got my gun out of my pocket and fired. I can't tell how many times I pulled the trigger, but think it was twice."

Twice or four times, it was enough. Champlin went out by the kitchen door, leaving it ajar, and walked downstairs to the outside rear door, which he closed (Dr. Streker had heard him close it). He jumped over a wire fence into the adjoining yard, crossed

Westminster Street and went through Howard to Broadway, backtracked to Carpenter and Fountain (which took him past police headquarters), reached Union Station, went into the men's room and washed up—"there was blood on the back of my right hand."

Then came an ironic period piece: "I then left the building and took a jitney to Broad Street." A jitney was a privately owned automobile (usually a Model-T Ford touring car) which its proprietor had converted into a common carrier by the simple expedient of putting a sign on it announcing its route and taking on any passengers who were willing to pay a nickel apiece for the ride. Allowing four passengers to each running board, he could squeeze on a dozen. The properly franchised transit corporations were at first annoyed by this phenomenon and then alarmed. What had begun as a nuisance had quickly developed into the source of a serious drain on their revenue. The time might come when every fourth or third citizen was operating his own transportation system. It took some time to legislate the jitneys out of existence, or into busses. For a high-ranking transit official like Champlin to patronize a jitney was tantamount to high treason. It was as if a W.C.T.U. executive had been detected staggering out of a saloon.

Champlin went to his rooming house, he said, reaching it just as a clock somewhere on the premises struck five. He took a bath "after heating the water myself." His confession continued:

"Both cuffs showed blood and I washed them out in the washbowl in the bathroom. There was some blood on the right sleeve above the cuff, which I also washed out. There was blood on the barrel of my revolver on one side and I wiped it off and cleaned out the barrel, as I had previously emptied out the revolver on Carpenter Street. I refilled it with ball cartridges in my bedroom, and put it in my overcoat pocket. I lay down on the bed, but did not sleep."

He left the house around seven-thirty in the morning and put in his usual day's work. But some time before nightfall he went back to the rooming house, got his gun, went down to the Crawford Street Bridge, at the head of navigation of Narragansett Bay, wrapped the gun in a handkerchief, and threw it into the water. The police later dragged for the gun but never found it; it is probably still under ten or fifteen feet of the odorous black silt that is the bed of the Providence River. A few days later the inevitable two small boys retrieved a gun, not Champlin's, from shallow water a good quarter of a mile from where Champlin's would have fallen.

Champlin also declared "that Leah C. Bishop was at no time aware or had any idea that I had any intention of any injury to or of going to call on Frederick H. Bishop, nor that I did go there last Sunday morning to kill her husband." Champlin had been employed by the trolley company for twenty years, he said. His wife had died two years previously—they had been married eighteen years. He had kept house himself for a time and then, responding to a classified advertisement, had gone to board with the Bishops, who were then operating a rooming house on Knight Street. The Bishops had moved to the apartment over Corrigan's drugstore at Westminster and Messer, and Champlin had taken a room on Central Street.

The medical examiner's findings did not altogether support Champlin's statement. "The condition of Bishop's bed indicated that the man was attacked while sleeping," declared the official. Of the four bullets fired, one had penetrated the left breast and was the proximate cause of death, one had lodged in the pelvis and one under the right ear, and one had grazed the hip and dropped to the floor.

On December 28, 1915—one month and one week after the crime—Champlin confronted Judge Elmer E. Rathbun in Supreme Court and pleaded *nolo contendere* to a charge of murder in the second degree. Attorney General Herbert A. Rice appeared for the prosecution, and Walter H. Barney, a court appointee, for the defense. Mr. Barney began with the time-tried apologia for the amateur murderer: "This man does not belong to the criminal class." He traced Champlin's early history—born on a farm in the South County, a sound common school education, a graduate of East Greenwich Academy. He came quickly to the confession. "No living eye saw what happened in that room except that of the defendant now before this bar. The array of circumstances against him was so great that I believe it my duty to advise him to make this plea, and say that he is unwilling to contend against the charge prepared by the state."

The Attorney General, not being limited by the proprieties to the boundaries of the confession, was more practical and less eloquent. He paid his respects to Mrs. Bishop—"from every standard of morality she was the instigator of that foul crime"— and continued: "Champlin went to the home of Bishop with the purpose of taking human life. With the key she had given him, he enters and crushes with a blackjack the head of his sleeping victim. The blow struck failed to produce immediate death, and Bishop sprang from his bed and attacked his assailant. Champlin draws his revolver and not once only but four times he empties the contents of its chambers into his victim, who falls back dead." Not back, but forward—and dead.

"This man's story of self-defense," Rice continued, "is an absolute falsehood. But I recognize the value of his services to the state in saving it the expense of a trial, and in view of this I was about to recommend a sentence less than life. But I realize that thousands are waiting to see what will be parcelled out to this evildoer. It is not within human power to impose a sentence adequate to the crime. For its deterrent effect upon others a severe sentence should be given. A man sentenced to prison for life has no hope. The prospect of freedom for a short time, even for a day only, might be a ray of hope. Perhaps the prisoner should have the chance of hope for freedom in view of his present attitude."

Rhode Island had abolished capital punishment half a century earlier after it had hanged the wrong man for murder. There is only one situation in which capital punishment can be invoked today, or could have been invoked in Champlin's day. If a prisoner who is serving a life sentence commits murder and is convicted of murder, he is liable to execution by hanging. This deadly combination of circumstances has never yet arisen.

Champlin stood up to receive the judgment of the court. Judge Rathbun asked him how old he was. "Forty-three," said Champlin. Judge Rathbun ordered him committed to state's prison for twenty-seven years, "thus fixing the date of the expiration of the sentence at the end of the allotted span of a man's life—three score and ten." This pious prospect was to be denied fulfillment.

Champlin may not have known or cared, but at that instant he became a landmark in Rhode Island's legal history. His was the first sentence for second-degree murder to be meted out since the founding of the state. The last previous legislature (Rhode Island legislatures seem to enjoy tinkering with the criminal laws, a predilection concerning which there will be more to say) had done away with the crime of manslaughter and had substituted for it the crime of murder in the second degree. The law had become effective September 9, 1915. The penalty provided was a minimum of ten years and a maximum of life imprisonment. To be sentenced to life imprisonment in Rhode Island for second-degree murder would be an ironic twist of fate, since one could enjoy the satisfaction and distinction of first-degree status and receive no heavier punishment.

Champlin was taken to the state penitentiary at Howard, a few miles south of Providence. In the normal course of events he would have served his sentence, with some time off for good behavior.

More than eleven years elapsed before Peleg Everett Champlin once more became front-page news. The state parole board met on April 28, 1927, and considered, among other matters, Champlin's request for parole "in order to join his eighty-five-year-old mother before she died." There was "a wide divergence of opinion" among members of the board, and Champlin did not get his parole. There was nothing against him on the record—nothing, that is, beyond a second-degree murder conviction—but the board stoutly resisted the temptation, all too frequently yielded to by individuals or groups with the power to parole or pardon, to turn a criminal loose because he has been a "model prisoner." Most one-shot murderers are model prisoners.

Champlin had received a far better education than most of his fellows—he was, one may hope for the sake of the good name of East Greenwich Academy, the only alumnus of that estimable institution in the state penitentiary; on the outside he had held a responsible position calling for the exercise of no little executive and administrative ability. A man so equipped is a prize in any penal institution—there is probably somewhere in the United States, at this very moment, at least one frantic prison warden who is chewing his fingernails in the desperate hope that some certified public accountant will obligingly go berserk. Champlin had been placed in charge of prison stores and records, and his duties took him outside the walled and barred confines of the prison proper into offices in which people who went home every night performed their daily stint at typewriter and adding machine and filing case. The door that led to the outer world was only a few feet distant. The idea of escape probably never entered his head, or, if it did, was as quickly dismissed. This had become his world, and of it he was no mean citizen.

In 1929, two years after the parole board had turned down Champlin's request, Warden Charles E. Linscott took Champlin to see his mother in the warden's own car.

Saturday was visiting day at the prison. Saturday, April 19, 1930, was a particularly busy visiting day. It was the eve of Easter. In Massachusetts it was Patriots' Day, celebrated throughout the commonwealth to honor the anniversary of Lexington and Concord. State boundaries are not matters of great moment in the lower strata of the criminal world—there were many visitors from Massachusetts that Saturday. It had been a long time since the penitentiary at Howard had played host to such a large company. As usual on a prison visiting day, women and children were in the majority.

Still, there were enough adult males present to make the entrance of two others, at about a quarter past two that afternoon, a not particularly conspicuous incident. One of the two told a clerk that he was a cousin of Thomas V. (Pretty) McNeal, who was serving thirty-five years for highway robbery. The two visitors wanted to talk to McNeal and to another prisoner, John Gilbert (Whitey) Miller, a bank robber who was also doing thirty-five years.

McNeal and Miller were summoned from the prison yard, where inmates were assembled subject to call during visiting periods. The pair went over to the prisoners' cage and greeted their two visitors. Between the outsiders and the insiders were two rows of bars some eight inches apart. Each row was covered with fine-mesh steel wire in order to discourage the transit of any material object from visitor to inmate—or, of less importance but not unimportant, vice versa.

While the four men were in conversation, a prison guard

and deputy turnkey named George McVay inserted a key into the outer of the two gates, also barred and meshed, which led from the visitors' room to the interior of the prison. He was some time about the business—perhaps the key stuck. One of the two visitors, neurotically impatient, or perhaps thinking that by now the gate must certainly be unlocked, brought the butt of a gun down several times on McVay's head. McVay managed to turn to face his assailant, who thereupon discharged the weapon point-blank into McVay's chest. McVay collapsed, desperately wounded.

The two visitors managed to turn the key and to get the outside gate open. McNeal began shooting at the lock of the inside gate. Where he had got the gun was a mystery. Today the usual method of getting small arms inside a prison is to wire them under the chassis of cars or trucks. Some day it may be compulsory for any vehicle entering a prison to halt at an inspection pit. But however McNeal obtained the gun, he had it and he was using it.

The crowd of authentic visitors was by now creating a pandemonium that must have all but drowned out the gunfire. Those who had first thought of it were flat on their faces under tables, chairs, benches; others were in rotating huddles whereof each member was attempting to get the others between himself or herself and the smoking gates.

Champlin, following the noon meal, had been about his lawful occasions in the prison offices. Hearing the shots and the tumult, he had rushed to the visitors' room, and, knowing its geography intimately, sized up the situation at a glance. But it required no special knowledge of prison geography for him to realize that desperate deeds were in the doing and that help was needed. Champlin ran to the main door, beside which hung the cord which sounded the prison siren. The freedom he was not seeking was a yard away. He grabbed the cord and pulled. From outside the door a gun blazed. Champlin fell dead, a slug through his heart. A little late, he had plumped valiantly for law and order.

A car quickly drove off with at least two men in it—probably more. No one paid it much attention—there was plenty going on inside the prison. Warden Linscott, unarmed, rushed from his quarters to the waiting room. As he opened the door he was confronted by a man with a gun who fired at him from a distance of ten inches. The hammer merely clicked. Linscott ran. A bullet nicked the wall beside him. He reached his office safely, picked up a gun, and ran back to the visitors' room.

The scene of battle inside the gate had now shifted. Guards were slowly forcing McNeal and Miller back. The siren Champlin had sounded brought Chief James G. Miller of the Cranston police force with several men—eventually thirty members of the force came to Howard. Miller called the Providence police, and Superintendent William F. O'Neil (who, as a chief inspector, had had charge of the investigation of the Bishop murder case) sent fifty men. Twenty-five state troopers arrived. What had looked like a good time to break out of Howard turned into the worst time in its history.

McNeal and Miller—only McNeal was armed—retreated to the prison barber shop. Miller went in first, to find the room already occupied. Thelma Linscott, the warden's twenty-three-year-old daughter, had been trapped in the prisoners' cage when the gunplay opened. She had run for safety to the barber shop.

Miller was chivalry itself. "Pardon me, lady, I didn't know you were in here," he said, and stepped aside to let her pass. She made her way unmolested to her father's office.

The police let loose with a riot gun and pitched tear-gas bombs into the barber shop. (Thelma was still near enough to get a whiff or two of the gas. The following day, despite the ordeal, she played the organ at the Easter services in the women's reformatory.)

A voice—Miller's—called out in surrender. He had been wounded in the leg. McNeal was dead. Miller had urged surrender, he later declared. "Nothing doing," McNeal had replied. "With thirty-five years ahead of me and a dead guy out there?" He put his gun to his temple and fired. (That morning McNeal had arranged to have Easter lilies sent to his mother.) By "dead guy" McNeal probably meant McVay. McVay, at the moment, was still alive. He died three days later, certain to the end that he would get well—so certain that he refused to make an ante-mortem declaration, which would have been valid in court, but in which he would have had to express the conviction that he was at the point of death.

Three arrests were made during the next few days, but the grand jury refused to indict. The prohibition interlude was at its wildest and wettest; everywhere the air was filled with the fumes of alcohol and gunpowder. Crime was organized with an effectiveness that was not to be equalled until Heinrich Himmler attained the height of his power. Its roots were dug deep, and the unlovely tree that grew out of them had many branches and a multitude of twigs.

Champlin's body was taken to the home of his eighty-eight-year-old mother. Four days after the Howard battle he was buried in Riverbend Cemetery at Westerly.*

Champlin's mother derived what satisfaction she could from a citation which concluded the report of an investigation conducted by the State Public Welfare Commission:

"We wish at this time to state that through the heroic efforts of Peleg Champlin, the general alarm was sounded, and through

---

* From a national point of view the attempted jail break at Howard quickly became small potatoes, for two days later, while Champlin was still above ground, inmates of the Ohio State Penitentiary at Columbus, in an effort to escape, set fire to the prison, and 318 fellow-prisoners were burned to death.

the loyalty and co-operation of other employees and trusties was a greater tragedy averted."

The commission also announced "certain contemplated changes in the entrance to the State Prison. It is planned to make a reception room out of the present archway by walling up both sides." This plan was carried out. In this reception room visitors are now liable to search at the discretion of the warden.

The case remained open. The Twenty-first Amendment was adopted, terminating the "noble experiment" initiated by the Eighteenth. The big-time crooks were driven into other fields of activity, and the small-time crooks, most of them, disappeared or went straight or starved to death. Then, in February, 1944, out of the clearest of skies, came what looked like a break in the Champlin case. One Walter Sullivan was arrested in Easton, Pennsylvania, on a vagrancy charge. It was not a good year in which to be a vagrant, a fact which may have troubled Sullivan's conscience. For whatever reason, or for no reason at all, he volunteered the fact that he had been implicated in the attempted break at the Rhode Island State Penitentiary.

Back in 1930 he had been a small-time hoodlum (and he had never got much forrader), a second-class private in the armies of gangsterdom. He had never been in Rhode Island in his life. With an associate who had also previously been denied that privilege, he was brought to Providence by a go-between and introduced to Raymond L. S. Patriarca. Patriarca, then twenty-two years old, had an impressive set of police statistics to his credit. Between 1926 and 1930 he had been arrested twenty-six times and convicted of a dozen offenses, among the least of which was dicing on Sunday—five dollars and costs. He had been paroled in Massachusetts, a civility which had rocked that politically minded commonwealth to the foundations of Boston State House, and which had brought about the impeachment of Attorney General Daniel H. Coakley. Patriarca, according to

Sullivan, took him and his companion over the getaway route from the prison—without, apparently, disclosing much information on any subject other than the topography of northern Rhode Island. Sullivan said the other out-of-state recruit was Johnny McLaughlin, who in 1930 had been eighteen years old. McLaughlin was now in the Army. He was stationed at Bolling Field, in the District of Columbia. The police brought him to Providence, and both Sullivan and McLaughlin were indicted for murder.

On September 24, 1944, when he reported to a parole officer, Patriarca was arrested and indicted on the charge of being an accessory before the fact to the murders of Champlin and McVay. An indictment was also returned against Joseph Fisher, an Alcatraz graduate who was serving out a twenty-five-year sentence in Leavenworth federal prison for a mail-robbery conviction. Patriarca pleaded not guilty.

Nine months later, on June 26, 1945, both indictments were invalidated. Nowhere under the law does the statute of limitations nullify a murder indictment. Perhaps only in Rhode Island does the statute of limitations operate in favor of a person charged with being an accessory before the fact of murder. The state legislature, once more tinkering with the criminal laws, had neglected to specify that accessory before the fact of murder may be as grave a crime as murder itself—that Lady Macbeth was as blood-soiled as her killer lord. The Supreme Court of Rhode Island took the legislature at its word, and Patriarca reverted to his parole status. Joseph Fisher's was more or less a purely moral victory. He stayed in Leavenworth.

What was behind the attempted jail delivery? Thugs do not risk their lives on behalf of their incarcerated fellows solely to let the latter draw a breath of free air, or in order to get experts to do a job—there are always enough experts on the outside. The most likely theory is that McNeal and Miller, with unspent loot tucked away somewhere, were willing to pay well for their freedom. It was a straight business proposition—a contract, without a penalty clause, on which the contractor was unable to deliver.

A few of the tag ends of the case were tied up, in the passage of time.

Walter Sullivan, the talker, was declared insane and committed to the state asylum, which is also at Howard.

Whitey Miller died in prison in 1943. In his later years he took up painting.

The murder indictment against Johnny McLaughlin was reduced to manslaughter, and Attorney General John E. Nolan (who was extremely bitter about that statute of limitations business, and said so) allowed McLaughlin to plead *nolo contendere* and released him on a deferred sentence to the Army Air Forces. McLaughlin's commanding officer was present to speak on McLaughlin's behalf had it been necessary to do so.

Peleg Champlin was not such a bad soldier either. I myself can testify to his high competence as a street-railway company inspector. I can also bear witness to Fred Bishop's competence as a motorman.

XVIII

One Bell

I AM now considerably more than twice the age at which I turned in my fare-collector and transfer-punch, and rather more than four times the age at which I delivered groceries for Benjamin Rich. So, for the sake of auld lang syne, whenever I visit Providence I like to explore the areas in which, at one time or another, I was listed on a payroll, and to see what they look like.

The premises where Benjamin Rich operated his tiny grocery, when I last saw them, were occupied by Posner's Shoe Rebuilding Service. The place was quite literally humming with industry.

Benjamin Green's haberdashery has been replaced (not without a struggle, I hope) by the Penn Hat Shop, an establishment catering to females exclusively. At least it is not a "shoppe." It announces, in neon lights, that it has the "smartest hats in town." I am not competent to sit in judgment on this claim.

The Outlet has spread all over the place. It must now equal in size some of the big department stores in New York, Chicago, and Philadelphia—and in Boston, a center always to be watched closely and jealously by Providence merchants. If the whole store had grown as amazingly as Department AA, the city itself could hardly contain it. The AA of my day embraced (and pretty snugly) a few hundred square feet; the extent of today's AA would have to be expressed in acreage. But they still call it AA, as I suppose they do in department stores all over the country, as well as in London, Prague, and Athens (where it is probably Alpha Alpha). The whole store has been prettied up and, as it were, bent into curves—the old-fashioned stores with sharp corners on the showcases, and straight lines joining the corners, seem to have vanished universally during the streamlining era, save in the instance of the dime stores, in which it is still possible to be directed to Counter 12, and even to find it. But I think I was still able to make out the suspended office where the Outlet's superintendent used to observe the scene below him like Dewey on the bridge of the *Olympia*.

The George W. Dover Company no longer exists as a corporate entity (but there is a George W. Dover, Jr., who sells insurance). The Dover building still stands, which is something it can well boast about, because most of the structures around it, decrepit enough in my day, have been torn down and the land on which they stood turned into parking lots. This tends to give the building the appearance of a tooth which the dentist decided to leave in place against his better judgment. At first glance the area does not seem to be so solidly devoted to jewelry making as it once was. Plumbing-supply houses, paint shops, riggers, ships' chandleries, and other mavericks have crowded in. But a closer inspection reveals that there are probably more manufacturing jewelers there than ever—tiny establishments that occupy little space. And there are half a dozen chromium platers—a calling unknown to my generation.

The waterfront below the jewelry area is now not so much a waterfront as a gasolinefront. In all my days I have seen no phenomenon more bizarre than the old wharf where the *Mount Hope* tied up now crammed with automobiles to the end of the stringpiece. Along this stretch of the Providence River the shoreline is an almost continuous stretch of parking lots, or parking piers.

The Providence Public Market is quieter than it used to be,

The Providence waterfront is now a gasolinefront.

largely because the old chute that once sluiced groceries up to the shipping room no longer exists. In fact, the shipping room no longer exists. There is a sort of vestigial shipping room in one corner of the main floor, with goods packed in cardboard cartons ready to be taken out. The market delivers now only to hospitals and hotels. Moreover, about half the main floor is divided off into a serve-yourself area. The door that led to the cutting room is still in place, however, and I suppose it still leads to the cutting room.

Classical High School used to have a few scatter-rugs of green grass around it, but these have now been concreted over to provide parking spaces for teachers' cars, I presume. Parking seems to have become Providence's major industry.

The Providence Gas Company's office has moved from North Main Street to a new (to me) building on lower Weybosset Street. Meter reading, as I have related, is now performed by full-time professionals, and I have no idea how students get through college these days.

The area in Olneyville in which I took census looks rather more like its 1910 self than I should have expected. I believe I was able to pick out the house in which the mill hand and his wife were rearing fifteen children. It has been repainted.

The radical who installed mercury-vapor lamps in the Providence Post Office has been overtaken and sunk, apparently, because the interior of the place is now illumined by ordinary incandescent bulbs inside white shades. On my last visit the post office lobby offered almost as many glass-cased exhibits as a small museum. In one of the cases were the likenesses, full front and profile, of thirteen wanted men (none of them of local origin, I was happy to observe) and also a "Warning: Do Not Be Defrauded by Spanish Swindle"; after Lord knows how many decades, or perhaps centuries, the old Spanish prisoner racket still seems to thrive hardily. Another case contained a list of anchorage regulations in Narragansett Bay (with charts), and an appeal by the Veterans Administration for sealed bids on "shears, hedge, blade 10", quantity six," and "shears, pruning, blade 9", quantity two"—swords into plowshares. Oddly, the table of restrictions on the hunting of migratory game birds usually found in urban post offices was not present.

Providence City Hospital, now the Charles V. Chapin Hospital, is two or three times the size it was when I became one of its first patients. It is no longer exclusively a hospital for contagious diseases, but takes on all comers.

I have never revisited Providence without taking a ride on a trolley car (or the closest available approximation). A few authentic trolley cars remain, but the city is now almost completely abandoned to a ridiculous artifact known as the trackless trolley. The Rhode Island Company has changed its name to United Electric Railways, which is a loud laugh, if a somewhat hollow one. No rails at all lead into the Elmwood and Cranston barns, which were among the largest; the Arlington carhouse is now occupied by the Fruehauf Trailer Company and the Pee Wee Brake and Frame Service; the immense (as they seemed to me once, and still do) repair shops on Cranston Street are now an appendage of the Narragansett Brewing Company.

The Olneyville carhouse is food for tears. The Hedge & Mattheis Company (pumps and hoists) has one end of it. Great Scott, the Better Super Market (dispensing, I suppose, neater, sweeter, cleaner, greener vegetables) has the other. This store appears to be the smallest in the Great Scott chain, and is probably known, in the company's books, as Little Great Scott, or Least Scott. Behind the carbarn I saw parked half a dozen appalling juggernauts labelled "Porter Trucking Company," so I suppose the Porter people have some unholy affiliation with the sacred premises. Each Porter truck was three times the size of the eight-bench bloomer that was the delight of my young manhood.

Trolley-car conductors, of course, disappeared long ago, well ahead of streetcar tracks. (What became of all the conductors? They were of no use as scrap metal.) The introduction of the pay-as-you-enter car made the motorman a solitary, wholly unenviable figure, with no one to talk to or to fight with.

With the conductor, of course, vanished the open car. And with the disappearance of the open car a romantic era in transportation closed. But unless they have open cars in Heaven I shall not enjoy the place.

Whenever I board a Providence streetcar I study the lone-wolf motorman with mingled expectancy and trepidation—in the hope of encountering an old familiar face, and in the fear of not quite knowing what I am to do about it when I do encounter one. "Oh, sure, sure, *I* remember you," lies the ancient. "So you're in New York now? Like it? Things are just about the same here. Who? Hell, he passed on along back before the war—the first war. Ain't many of the real old crowd left. Me, and So-and-so, and Such-a-one (naming half a dozen unrecognizables who probably began collecting fares ten years after my day)—that's about all. No, you pay when you leave now, and it's eight cents. Or you can get five tokens for thirty-five cents."

But oftener, far oftener, the man at the handles or the wheel is a stranger and a child, to whom the heart utters unspoken words:

"Youth, you were born too late ever to be young. Whatever run they give you, the route lies downhill. I railroaded when the streetcar circled the summit. *You* can never experience the thrill even of riding in, let alone of operating, a bloomer. Man never devised a transportation medium endowed with nobler potentialities for delight. What can you know of the joys of the open road who never have known and never shall know the joys of the open car?"

On each of these excursions into the past I scan the front of every operator's hat to see if anybody is wearing my old number —642. I have never found him. All in the valley of Death ride the six hundreds.

XIX

Postscript: Home-Town Stuff

ALL work and no play may well make a dull book. So, as an antidote to industry, I shall conclude these notes with a chronicle that is relevant solely by reason of its irrelevancy. Here, then, is a tale of money not being earned, but being spent—a tale set not in a New England industrial city, but in a pleasant, vine-clad countryside bordering a river that twists in fantastic loops to meet the Rhine.

During the early weeks of 1945, I expected almost any day to read in the newspapers the heartening but embarrassing intelligence that an American armored spearhead had captured Winterich-an-der-Mosel. This dingy, down-at-heel hamlet (it was dingy and down-at-heel in 1927, and I see no ground for supposing that it has improved in the interval) was the place from which my emigrating paternal grandfather got his name and passed it along to me. Winterich did get captured in General Patton's great fanning-out movement to the right after he reached Coblenz, but his bag was so extensive that there was no room on the cables for the listing of not-so-wide spots in the road. Anyway, Patton's object, quite properly, was not the seizure of real estate but the destruction of hostile armies.

American troops had held Winterich-an-der-Mosel before. They were there, and a dull time they must have had, during the occupation of the Coblenz bridgehead from the end of 1918 on to whenever-it-was. Throughout their tenure, the name of Winterich-an-der-Mosel did not, so far as I am aware, appear in the headlines.

All through that other war, and particularly during the eighteen months I myself spent overseas, I lived in a state of palpitating apprehension lest a Winterich on the wrong side of the fence commit some vast indiscretion that would bring a fair name into disrepute. The closest approach to any such disaster came with the appointment to the German armistice delegation of an old-school Prussian general named von Winterfeldt—a designation, lacking the "von," which harried department-store salespersons have once or twice affixed to delivery tags on my purchases. Not until many years after the war did I learn that my near-namesake had indeed committed that vast indiscretion which, had the perpetrator been a Winterich and had the story become public at the time, would have turned me crimson with shame. I had the story from an American who had served in the French Army as an officer on the staff of General Mangin. Mangin got it direct from Foch.

When the German armistice delegates entered the fateful dining car in the Forest of Compiègne, General von Winterfeldt, with taste incredibly bad even for a Prussian general, was wearing on his tunic the cross of the Legion of Honor. That was too much for Foch. He strode over to von Winterfeldt, removed the decoration, and put it in his own pocket. "That," Foch later told Mangin, "is my only war souvenir."

I asked my informant how in the world von Winterfeldt had earned the Legion of Honor. "A year or two before the war, the French put on a big military aviation show at Pau," he told me. "Anyway, it was big for that day. Von Winterfeldt was then German military attaché at Paris and attended in his official capacity. A grandstand collapsed and von Winterfeldt got a broken leg—and the Legion of Honor."

Von Winterfeldt died in troubled retirement during the

Second World War. I recall breathing easier when I read the inconspicuous notice that signalled his passing; I should have nothing more to fear from him. I wish I could say as much for the Winteriches. For there is one Winterich about whom I still have grave doubts.

My German-born grandfather died in Georgia in 1867, as I have related, when my father was two years old. The ties that bind me to the Rhineland, therefore, are extremely tenuous. But for as long as I can remember, I naturally had a sentimental interest in it and always hoped that I might one day visit it. That opportunity came in the spring of 1919, when I spent a few days in occupied Germany, chiefly at Coblenz and Cologne. My train passed through Trier without stopping, which was a disappointment, because Winterich is one of the villages which surround Trier, and because it was from Trier, his birthplace, that my grandfather had set out to make his way in the new world.

I remember that at Coblenz, in 1919, I explored a city directory and found several Winteriches listed there. Suggesting to a fellow-soldier named Ross that he accompany me on a round of visits to these Winteriches (the nonfraternization regulation was off the books by this time), I was met by the retort that he was not interested in watching me converse with a swarm of eighth cousins in sign language. He added that I might not be altogether socially acceptable in the guise of a conquering hero.

Both these arguments were unanswerable. My German was, and is, of the most rudimentary. From my father I had learned half a dozen songs, the alphabet, and the cardinal numbers up to ten. Armed with this meagre equipment, I went to college and began my compulsory course in elementary German under the illusion that any truck with textbooks would be supererogatory and silly. I flunked the course handsomely and had to repeat it. During the repetition I did study, but with a loathing so lusty

The proprietor of the gasthaus was constructed like an All-American end.

that it enabled me to forget everything I learned as soon as it had served its purpose of getting me by.

I have forgotten, too, the instructor's name, but he was tall, spare, mustached, bespectacled, and something of a wag. On one occasion we were about to take on a new textbook, a collection of stories by Gottfried Keller, and we were simultaneously moving to a new classroom in the basement.

"Morgen," said the instructor, with a guttural chuckle, *"morgen lesen wir Keller im Keller."* That is the only joke in German I know. Perhaps it is the only joke in German there is.

Well, I decided not to visit any Winteriches in Coblenz. I attempted to speak German there only once. Ross and I entered a café. It was midspring, the season of *Maiwein,* that sweet, sticky, spicy, and altogether mild and innocent concoction, served, if memory does not betray me, warm. We sat at a table. A waiter approached. Now was to be my moment of triumph. Sign language, indeed!

"Bitte?"

"Deux wein."

Not until eight years later did I set foot in Trier and Winterich and meet in the flesh any untransplanted Germans who bore my own name. By that time I was married, and Emily, my wife, who happened to have been born in Austria, spoke a German which, though rusty from disuse, was adequate for all impractical purposes. For example, if I said, "Find out if the ten thirty-five for Berlin carries a diner," her tongue would cleave to the roof of her mouth. Ten minutes after the train started, however, she would be in voluble conversation with the mother of three tow-headed youngsters or with a Cologne businessman, commuting to his home in Düsseldorf, who was maintaining, with no great vehemence, that America should have kept out of the war.

However, Emily and I reached Trier, on a quiet September evening, without too great a strain on her German. A cab bore us through dimly lighted streets to the Hotel Porta Nigra, opposite which the Black Gate itself, sturdy relic of Rome's ancient overlordship of Europe, loomed solidly in the night. We arranged for a taxi to call for us the following morning to carry us the twenty-five kilometres to Winterich, for it appeared that the ancestral acres were not on the railroad. .

The taxi turned out to be one of those incredibly decrepit affairs which operate largely on the unassailable faith of their drivers. Our driver was of a piece with his vehicle, but quieter. The road led out into the country, past terraced hillsides on which the vineyards stretched like festoons of camouflage. There is no spot on earth where the grape is cultivated more intensively. These Moselle vineyards were flourishing when the slopes of the Rhine itself were dark forest to the water's edge and the Roman sentry on the left bank gazed awesomely eastward into terra incognita. And while my own preference is a Pommard or a Chablis, I am liberal in these matters and have never turned down a glass of a Berncasteler Doktor.

An hour's gentle jolting brought Emily and me to the river's edge at a point where a whitewashed flatboat was moored. This, it appeared, was the ferry that was to carry us over to Winterich. I was relieved to learn that the taxi would wait for us on the northern bank. A steel cable reaching from shore to shore passed through rings affixed to poles at the ends of the craft, and the operator, who was even less loquacious than the taxi driver (which means that, for lack of evidence to the contrary, he might actually have been dumb), poled us across. The river was barely fifty yards wide and there seemed to be next to no current. The passage was without incident.

I set foot in Winterich for the first (and so far for the last) time with an accelerated pulse and quivering nostrils, the latter phenomenon induced by a pervasive odor of cow dung. Its ubiquitous cowness remains to this day my great inclusive recollection of Winterich. Though it might be in the heart of a famous wine country, Winterich evidently put its trust in a milder and more elemental tipple.

It took us less than five minutes to pass Winterich's half-dozen houses and get to the other end of town along a dusty road over which no other traffic was moving. The final evidence of the hand of man, before fields and woods took over, was a small, walled-in, overgrown cemetery with a locked iron gate. It could not have been more than an acre in extent, but if this were indeed God's acre, he was paying little enough attention to it. Tall weeds held full sway. Such tombstones as were visible through the tangle were askew and illegible. I decided that if any ancestors of mine were laid away in this unkempt and desolate spot, then so far as I was concerned their rest would remain unbroken. We walked back toward the ferry.

So far we had seen no living soul, but now a black-smocked urchin appeared from nowhere, and, after gazing at us for some moments in a mixture of contempt, curiosity, and distrust, directed us, in response to our inquiry, to the residence of the *Bürgermeister*. It was a far from imposing structure, even though it was rather larger than any of its handful of neighbors.

A pleasant, fresh-faced *Hausfrau* came to the door, wiping her hands on her apron. *"Bitte?"* she said.

"Good morning," Emily began in German. "My man is called Winterich and we have come to see the village from which he takes his name. We are Americans."

"Bitte, bitte," said the *Frau Bürgermeister,* smiling and motioning us within.

We entered a narrow passageway that sliced the building in half. Judging by the sudden stepping-up of the cow-dung odor the instant we entered, I suspected that the half on the left was a stable. The room on the right into which we were ushered was obviously a little-used salon which, save for the fact that it was much smaller, almost exactly duplicated the rural New England parlor of my childhood. The floor was covered by a carpet which, when new, must have been hideous in its garishness; time and wear had somewhat subdued its huge red flowers. There was a scarred upright piano topped by a dark velours drape which gave the ensemble the aspect of a sarcophagus. On a table stood a porcelain lamp, with a globe covered with more huge red flowers, and there were three chairs with green plush seats.

Would we seat ourselves, *bitte, bitte,* and we did, most un-comfortably. No, said the *Frau Bürgermeister,* there was no Win-terich in the village. The last of that name had left long before her time. (I did not say so, but I thought they had been well ad-vised. At least a yearning for something better characterized the family strain.) But, she went on, there were Winteriches in Trier.

I had been mildly put out by the fact that the few road signs I had noticed on the way to the village, and in the village itself, had read "WINTRICH." I am against simplified spelling on prin-ciple and I certainly am against having it applied to my own name. The *Frau Bürgermeister* said that the alteration went back to her girlhood, but was unable to account for it. She evi-dently did not care one way or the other. Right then I began to develop misgivings about the future of this new Germany. If higher authority could tinker indiscriminately with place names and nobody gave a damn, the process might go on indefinitely and more radical alterations might be put into effect and ac-cepted with equal complacency.

We talked inconsequentialities—that is, Emily and the *Frau Bürgermeister* talked them—for ten minutes lavishly sprinkled with *bitte, bittes.* A German can do a lot with a single *bitte* and more than twice as much with two. The double-barrelled *bitte* can be anything from the mark of cringing servility to the solicitous interrogation of an equal. It was in the latter sense that the *Frau Bürgermeister* used it. She was a pleasant person. However, if she is still alive, I am sure she is still convinced that it was the Communists who set fire to the Reichstag.

We took our leave, went down to the river bank, boarded the whitewashed flatboat, and were soon in our creaking cab on the way back to Trier. We were at the outskirts of the city when the big moment came.

"Look!" cried Emily, pointing to a huge gray stone building ahead. On the front wall, just above the ground-floor windows, was painted, in black Gothic letters a yard high, *GASTHAUS WINTERICH*.

Our cab had trundled a hundred feet beyond this noble edifice before it occurred to me to call on the driver to stop. Besides, I did not know how to make a cab stop in German and had to ask Emily to help. She got it not only to stop but to back up, which was as great a feat mechanically as linguistically.

The *Gasthaus Winterich* was at the end of a streetcar line, and I suppose residents of the city often indulged in the mild dissipation of riding out for a glass of beer of an evening. I was tremendously impressed. This was the first saloon I had ever heard of in the family and I was delighted to find that it was such a big one.

We went in. The interior was cool and dark. There was about the premises a pleasant savor of beer and tobacco. The air circulated freely through open doors and windows, and the smell was not the stale stench of the morning after but a clean, honest, ingrained aroma with a tradition behind it. There may never have been high thinking in these agreeable purlieus, but I am sure there was, or had been, good drinking, hearty eating, and zestful song. It did not seem, at the moment, an ideal setting for a beer-hall putsch.

The room was deserted. Not one of the tables, each of which had its clean white cloth, was occupied. One explanation of this was the fact that it was three-thirty in the afternoon. Presently footsteps sounded behind a partition and a figure came into view.

The proprietor of the *Gasthaus Winterich* was impressive to look upon. He was perhaps twenty-five years old, six feet tall, and constructed like an All-American end. Though he wore a plain gray jacket and trousers, his black puttees gave him the appearance of being in uniform. I have never been able to figure out the reason for the puttees—they were hardly *de rigueur* for the proprietor of a *Gasthaus*.

Nor have I been able to account for the fact that he was accompanied by the largest German shepherd dog I have ever seen. He was holding the dog firmly by a very short leash, six inches or so long, as if the creature would otherwise be at our throats. Of the two, however, the dog certainly appeared to be the more amiable. The dog looked at us with inquiry but not with hostility. He did not growl or show his teeth. Neither, exactly, did his owner, but I expected him to at any instant. The man was smooth-shaven, tight-lipped, unsmiling, as far removed as might be from the good-natured host he ought to have been if he knew what was good for business. After all, he did not yet know that we were not customers.

Plainly the burden of the discourse was going to be on us, meaning Emily. She asked him if his name was Winterich and he said yes, with the air of its being forced from him under oath. She then explained once more that her man was also called Winterich and that the grandfather of her man had gone to America from Trier. The other Winterich nodded austerely and let his face unfreeze into the suggestion of a formal smile. He said that was interesting, and tossed the ball back to us. I told Emily to tell him he had a nice place here but that I would take the Hotel Porta Nigra any time. I later learned that she softened this in translation to the simple announcement that we were stopping at the Porta Nigra. (That is the worst of employing an interpreter. You are at his, or her, mercy.) The young man nodded and it was our turn again. Emily said we were happy to have met him. He bowed stiffly and I bowed back, trying to make my bow a little stiffer than his. We went out into the sunlight. Not a single *bitte* had changed hands.

Considerably chastened, we returned to the hotel and paid off the driver, whose parting *"Danke schön"* about doubled his conversation for the whole trip. The local Winteriches were a dour lot, we decided. We had a late lunch, or, rather, a high *Kaffeeklatsch,* and so did not get around to wanting dinner until nine that evening.

In the middle of the meal I was startled to hear my name called by the stout, elaborately uniformed commissionaire, who told me I was wanted on the telephone. It was the first time I had ever been called Herr Winterich. Who would be wanting us in Trier? No one knew where we were and we did not know a soul nearer than Paris. If the call were long distance, a certain amount of discussion with a German telephone operator would be in order, so I grasped Emily by the hand and led her to the booth.

It proved to be the mother of the *Gasthaus* proprietor. Walther, or Hermann, or Kurt, or whatever his name was, had told her about us (I would give a good deal, even at this late date, to know exactly what he had said) and she was most anxious to meet us. We were leaving at eleven next morning for Paris? Could she send for us at nine-thirty?

Send what, we wondered? We found out at nine-thirty the

following morning when a Buick roadster stopped at the door of the Porta Nigra. It was driven by a sister of the proprietor of the *Gasthaus* (a sister a year or two younger, I surmised), and her brother was with her. She got out and introduced herself as Frau Somebody. Her husband was a wholesale wine dealer. She was friendly and pretty and modishly dressed, and she spoke excellent English. By this time a considerable crowd had gathered to admire the Buick. Our mere association with it made us persons of mark in Trier.

We got in the car, and in the process the most damnable maladjustment of seating arrangements was brought about. Emily and the sister, both of whom, remember, spoke German *and* English, were in the front seat, and the brother and I, who could not talk to each other in anything, had the rumble. Under ordinary circumstances, of course, one could hardly ask a lady to climb into a rumble when a front seat was available, but these were not ordinary circumstances. As a result, throughout our two-mile drive, Emily and the sister were in voluble conversation (in English), while the brother and I, impotent and tongue-tied, studied the scenery. Once I extended my case and said, "Cigarette?" He said no or *nein* or shook his head. That was our whole conversation.

The car drew up in front of an elaborate stone house directly at the right of the *Gasthaus*. We were shown to an upstairs living room, where Frau Winterich and her younger daughter, aged eighteen or thereabouts, greeted us. Introductions were made with as much informality as in Bronxville or Old Greenwich, and we were soon chatting away as if we were old friends met together after a few months' absence. The big shepherd, now off leash, wagged his tail. Even Walther (or Hermann or Kurt) unbent and grinned once or twice.

Frau Winterich, a widow in her middle fifties, genial and talkative, spoke no English. The younger daughter did, but not so fluently as the older. Thus, of the six in the party, five spoke German, four English, three German and English, two German only, and one English only. In spite of this moderate confusion of tongues, the conversation flowed smoothly, amicably, even gaily. The introduction of the family cognac bottle (reserved, I am sure, for state occasions) did nothing to hinder the process. I am not among those who regard the drinking of cognac at ten in the morning as one of the higher social graces, but exceptions may be made to any rule if conformity to hidebound convention would oppose the general comity.

Of our three-quarter-of-an-hour visit with the *Familie Winterich* I retain, after this interval, only these specific recollections:

(1) It was extremely doubtful that there was any blood tie between the cis- and trans-Atlantic Winteriches close enough to bother about.

(2) During the other war, when the Americans occupied Trier, two lieutenants were billeted in the house. Shown to a bedroom, they engaged in a debate (not knowing that anyone there understood English) as to whether they should sleep with their revolvers under their pillows and finally voted in favor of it.

(3) In Germany, as in France, Buick is a monosyllable. It rhymes with "quick."

Walther, or whoever he was, and the married daughter drove us to the railroad station under the same appalling seating arrangement as before. This time, however, I ignored Walther and beamed genially at the populace, which was popeyed over the Buick. Our trip to the station was a triumphal one-car procession.

A few months later, back in America, we had a letter, in English, from the married daughter. She hoped we had enjoyed our visit to Germany and our stay in Paris. All were well. They would be delighted to hear from us. We answered, also in English, and brought them up to date.

Three or four years afterward—in 1931, I think—another letter came, in German, from Walther. Things were not going so well. Living was expensive. The wine crop had been poor. Many were out of work. Would I care to buy the *Gasthaus Winterich* for thirty-five thousand reichsmarks?

It seemed cheap, but I said no. That closed the correspondence.

The foregoing narrative first appeared in *The New Yorker* for February 17, 1945, a few days before the Trier area fell to the advancing Americans. Some two months later I received a letter from Frank Smith of Greenwood, Mississippi (who at the moment was a captain in the 243rd Field Artillery Battalion), which supplies an interesting sequel to my own account. He wrote:

"Yesterday [April 2, 1945] I made a trip back into the area you describe, and detoured a few miles in order to pass through Winterich. I would say that there has been no change since your visit, other than the disappearance of all military-age men. Practically the entire population was on the street when I drove through, gathering at the church for the Easter Monday services. In Sunday clothes they did not appear to have suffered much from the war. Winterich was not important enough to receive attention from our Air Forces, and our armor drove through without stopping. Even the German Army must have failed to make its usual requisition of bicycles for retreat, for quite a few were in evidence. I notice that I have been misspelling the name of the village. There is still no *e*.

"Trier got a good working over from the Air Forces, and we shelled it for weeks, all through the Battle of the Bulge. But I found the Winterich tavern still intact, probably because of it fortunate location on the edge of town. All the windows were broken, but the building itself had not been damaged. The furnishings were a different story, smashed and strewn everywhere, upstairs and down. I would guess that most of the damage was done by German soldiers who both lived in the place and looted it. Parts of their uniforms and equipment were in evidence.

"Your 'cousin' may have succeeded in selling his business, for I could find no evidence of anyone named Winterich living there. The only shell (small calibre) to strike the building knocked off enough plaster from the front to leave 'terich' as the only legible part of the name Winterich, but I am sure I found the building you described. The enclosed list of residents posted on the door seems to bear out my assumption that the Winteriches had moved out."

The list of residents which Captain Smith enclosed was a roster of air-raid wardens, fire-watchers, and assistants at 24, 25, 26, and 27 Pallienerstrasse, Trier. They were Peter Winkel, Willi Linke, Angela Schmutz, Helene Winkel, Katharina Krämer, Hilda Beck, Anna Steffgen, and Franziska Linke. All are strangers to me.

Emily and I are going back some day and look the place over.